ENDORSEMENTS

"Carolyn Custis James has written an unusual and compelling book, mixing her personal story with the dramatic changes in today's world and her thoughtful interpretations of the Scriptures and how women can respond with greater fervor to the Bible's call for change and betterment of the world."

—**Sheryl WuDunn,** coauthor,
Half the Sky

"*Half the Church* is a significant contribution to the current public discourse of the role and responsibility of the church in responding to the suffering of millions of women and girls due to oppressive cultural and traditional norms. In her excellent book, Carolyn James reminds us of the urgent need for action in order to protect girls and women from gender-based violence and cultural practices such as trafficking, forced child-marriage, gang rapes, abduction, infanticide, and female genital mutilation."

—**Fatuma Hashi,** director, Gender
and Development, World
Vision International

"Once again Carolyn Custis James calls us to radical thinking and living. *Half the Church* opens our eyes to the global problems facing women, drives us to God as the only solution, and refreshes our passion that we can 'do something.' And the writer in me loves Carolyn's exquisite phrases and vibrant images. This book is a must-read and I will be giving it to many people."

—Judy Douglass, director of Women's
Resources, Campus Crusade

"In *Half the Church*, Carolyn Custis James offers a striking theology as to why men and women are called to live and lead together. Her insightful, integrated and unapologetic plea leaves us with no option but to *get on with it ... all* of us ... men and women *together* urgently working for God's best in this world."

—Elisa Morgan, author, speaker,
and publisher of *FullFill*

"With the care of an experienced scout, Carolyn James has lined the fire pit with stones, then assembled the kindling and logs, and in the final chapters of this remarkable book has struck the match to ignite a blaze for God and his kingdom. No thoughtful Christian woman can walk away from this book unchallenged or unmoved, as she senses the glory of her ezer-warrior calling. Nor can any thoughtful Christian man remain unmoved by the vision of the Blessed Alliance so skillfully sketched in these pages. The challenge of *Half the Church* is to the whole church to fulfill God's purpose in creating all of us as iconoclastic bearers of the divine image in a broken world."

—Alice Mathews, Gordon-Conwell
Theological Seminary

"Carolyn Custis James expertly weaves contemporary reality with biblical story. Reaching into the Old Testament as well as the New, Carolyn shows that God has always been and continues to be at work through women and girls. They are, like men and boys, His image bearers. This book should open the eyes of everyone who takes Jesus seriously to the horrendous injustices against women around the world and provoke within us a serious drive to do something about it. The day is near (and I believe this book will help usher it in) when the church will be a significant cultural catalyst for bringing equality and dignity to women and girls around the world by providing education, empowering women with microloans, and liberating them from oppressive regimes, sex trafficking circles, and secular philosophies that are ultimately degrading to them. It is time for the other half of the church, men, to be strong and courageous and do all we can with all we have to bring divine freedom to women and girls so they can be all that God created them to be."

—**Mark L. Russell,** coauthor,
Routes and Radishes

"Women hold up 'half the sky'—and maybe a bit more. Yet this very hour they are demeaned and destroyed, trafficked and exploited, everywhere in the world. James argues that it's time for the church to roll up its sleeves and do something about it. A compelling and inspiring book!"

—**Miroslav Volf,** author,
Allah: A Christian Response
and Henry B. Wright Professor of
Theology at Yale Divinity School

HALF THE CHURCH

Recapturing
GOD'S GLOBAL VISION
for Women

CAROLYN CUSTIS JAMES

ZONDERVAN

Half the Church
Copyright © 2011 by Carolyn Custis James

This title is also available as a Zondervan ebook. Visit www.zondervan.com/ebooks.

This title is also available in a Zondervan audio edition. Visit www.zondervan.fm.

Requests for information should be addressed to:

Zondervan, *Grand Rapids, Michigan 49530*

Library of Congress Cataloging-in-Publication Data

James, Carolyn Custis, 1948-.
    Half the church : recapturing God's global vision for women / Carolyn Custis
James.
        p.   cm.
    ISBN 978-0-310-32556-7 (hardcover, jacketed)
    1. Women in Christianity. 2. Women and religion. I. Title.
BV639.W7J36   2010
270.8'3082—dc22   2010038223

All Scripture quotations, unless otherwise noted, are taken from two versions:

The Holy Bible, *New International Version*®, *NIV*®. Copyright © 1973, 1978, 1984 by
Biblica, Inc.® Used by permission of Zondervan. All rights reserved worldwide.

The *Holy Bible, New Living Translation,* copyright © 1996, 2004. Used by permission of
Tyndale House Publishers, Inc., Wheaton, Illinois. All rights reserved

Published in association with the literary agency of Wolgemuth & Associates, Inc.

Cover design: Rob Monacelli
Interior design: Beth Shagene

Printed in the United States of America

---

13 14 15 16 17 18 19 20 /DCI/ 22 21 20 19 18 17 16 15 14 13 12 11 10 9 8 7 6 5 4

With love
to my cousin Karen Custis Wilson
who is better than a sister to me
and
to the women of Synergy—
a growing company of ezers-warriors who are
blessing the church and the world with their gifts.

CONTENTS

ACKNOWLEDGMENTS

Whenever I reach the finish line of another book manuscript, I am acutely mindful that I couldn't have made it here on my own. It may not take a village to write a book, but deep inside I know that in writing this book, I have been bolstered by the interaction and support of many friends and fueled by the bold honesty of some people I don't even know. God has blessed my journey, and from the bottom of my heart I thank him for the people he put in my life who have helped me along the way.

For truth-tellers like Amy Carmichael, Sheryl WuDunn and Nicholas Kristof, Diane Langberg, Gary Haugen, Greg Mortenson, and countless others who have shattered my belief that the world I experience is normal and have set an inescapable reality before me that continues to appall and that beckons me, as God's image bearer, to get involved;

For sisters in Christ (you know who you are) who tell me your stories of disappointment and loss, and of your passion for the kingdom of Jesus Christ. You are constant reminders of why I do what I do. You fill my heart with hope that the gifts God has entrusted to his daughters and the struggles we experience along the way will not be wasted but will be spent for his glory;

For friends like Amy Lauger, whose statistical expertise and careful eye contributed enormously to my research and whose late-night Facebook chats were welcome breaks from writing;

For academic friends — Mark Futato, Tremper Longman, and Roy Ciampa — who have taken time to engage and respond to my biblical and theological questions and who should not be held responsible for what I ultimately said in this book;

For partners in ministry like Elisa Morgan, publisher of *FullFill*™ (www.fullfill.org), who opened the door for me to develop and test drive some of these ideas and graciously gave me permission to reuse material previously published in *Full-Fill*'s {Think} column;

For advocates like Robert and Erik Wolgemuth, who do not merely see me through the early phase of securing a contract but accompany me to the finish line with their prayers, words of encouragement, and conviction that the work I'm doing is important;

For my friends at Zondervan — Katya Covrett, who isn't afraid to mix friendship with business and leaves no stone unturned when she gets behind an author; Verlyn Verbrugge, who has changed the sometimes painful final editing process into a positive experience for me; Jesse Hillman, whose creative efforts are finding ways to spread this message more widely; Rob Monacelli, who has a perfect batting average when it comes to designing book jackets (he is three for three for me); Beth Shagene for designing the internal layout;

For thoughtful readers — Dixie Fraley Keller, Susan Anders, Helen Chen, and Pamela Rossi-Keen — who combed through every chapter, interacted with my ideas, offered helpful suggestions, and gave lots of encouragement that I needed;

For prayer warriors like my parents, Dwight and Lucille Custis, whose love and daily intercession are, I am certain, what kept me going through dry stretches of writer's block and fatigue and low moments when I struggle under the weight of the suffering I am witnessing;

For my husband, Frank James, who gives new and deeper meaning to what it means to be "my BFF." You have walked with me every step of the way, not just in the thinking and writing of this book, but in all the others too. Every day with you, I learn more about what it means to be a Blessed Alliance and of the kingdom potency God embedded in male/female relationships when he created his first two image bearers.

THE INVENTION OF FRACTIONS

God created the whole numbers:
the first born, the seventh seal,
Ten Commandments etched in stone,
the Twelve Tribes of Israel —
Ten we've already lost —
forty days and forty nights,
Saul's thousand and David's ten thousand.
'Be of one heart and one mind' —
the whole numbers, the counting numbers.

It took humankind to need less than this;
to invent fractions, percentages, decimals.
Only humankind could need the concepts
of splintering and dividing,
of things lost or broken,
of settling for the part instead of the whole.

Only humankind could find the whole numbers,
infinite as they are, to be wanting;
though given a limitless supply,
we still had no way
to measure what we keep
in our many-chambered hearts.

— JESSICA GOODFELLOW[1]

SEEING
BEYOND OURSELVES

There is more to us than we know.
If we can be made to see it,
perhaps for the rest of our lives
we will be unwilling to settle for less.[1]

Sometimes when you're searching for answers, you get more than you bargained for. My search for answers began in earnest in the years after college when I landed in a stretch of singleness I didn't see coming that dragged on for years. It was the first of many chapters in my story where the plot read differently from what I was expecting and where I was pulled unwillingly into a struggle with God and into questions about my purpose as a woman. I've been asking questions ever since.

I am not alone. Other women are asking hard questions too. The reality that we are living in a fallen world confronts us every day. Still, we can't help wondering why God is silent when that brokenness invades our lives. Every day we are bombarded with new questions as the twenty-first century hurtles forward at a wild speed that has everyone hanging onto their hats and scrambling to keep up with the changes. During the latter half of the twentieth century, doors swung open for women (some after significant effort) that had been bolted shut for previous generations. In her book *When Everything Changed: The Amazing Journey of American Women from 1960 to the Present*,[2] *New York Times* op-ed columnist Gail Collins escorts the reader on a mind-boggling journey from the 1960s to the present and examines the revolutionary changes that women in America currently enjoy and that young women today simply take for granted. In many ways for so many Western women, it is an exciting time to be alive.

Yet at the same time, like a nagging cough, the same old problems have traveled with us into this new era and leave us wondering if some things will ever change. Questions and uncertainty over a woman's identity, purpose, and calling persist. We are constantly bewildered over God's mysterious ways and unnerved by his silence when we need him most. And, of course, the ongoing struggles between the sexes have a sticking power that seems to resist our best attempts to resolve them.

It is perhaps ironic that in the twenty-first century we are looking for answers in an ancient Middle Eastern book—a book produced in a society that is alien to our postmodern Western world in time, culture, and a million other ways. But as Christians we owe it to ourselves and to our daughters to find out if the ancient message for women in the Bible is still relevant in the twenty-first century or if, as many suggest, we have outgrown its message. Does God's vision for his daughters equip us to move boldly into the future or summon us to retreat into the past? Does it break down when things go wrong for us, or is it robust enough to remain intact no matter what happens? Is his vision big enough to include every woman's story from the beginning to the final chapter?

These questions have propelled my work. Listening to the questions of other women and girls has stretched the parameters of my search, for although I am passionate about finding answers for myself, I can't put my weight down on answers that collapse under other women's stories. It also became apparent to me early on that this conversation is dangerously incomplete and certain to produce flawed conclusions if we exclude our sisters in other cultures around the world. The conversation about God's vision isn't American or Western or middle class. It is global. I knew that going in.

Even though the journey has been agonizing for me at many points, I wouldn't trade those eye-widening moments of discovery for anything, and I have had many. The winding path of questions eventually led me to a rich, wide-open space where God is spreading before his daughters a vast global vision that frees us to follow wherever he leads.

The thrill of each new discovery has been tempered every time by a weight of grief that to this day hasn't lifted. I grieve over the opportunities and blessings I have wasted because I didn't know about God's vision for his daughters—I didn't realize God expected so much of me. I grieve the loss to the church when so many Christian women believe it's possible to subsist on an anorexic spiritual diet. I grieve that far too many women and girls are living with small visions of themselves and of their purpose. I grieve the loss to our brothers who are shouldering burdens we were created to share and are doing kingdom work without us when God means for us to build his kingdom together.

When half the church holds back—whether by choice or because we have no choice—everybody loses and our mission suffers setbacks. Tragically, we are squandering the opportunity to display to an embattled world a gospel that causes *both* men and women to flourish and unites us in a Blessed Alliance that only the presence of Jesus can explain. Grief in me created a burning in my bones because we are not trumpeting this message within our ranks and to those outside. I knew I had to do something.

A trilogy of books—*When Life and Beliefs Collide*, *Lost Women of the Bible*, and *The Gospel of Ruth*—chronicle my journey and the discoveries I have made along the way. Each book led me deeper in my search into the Scriptures and opened up more of God's ever-widening vision for his daughters. The book you hold in your hand is the fourth. But it is different from the others and requires a bit of explaining.

At first my purpose in writing this book was simply to put into a single volume the ideas that were simmering and evolving in those first three books but are scattered in different chapters. Much as I hope others will take that journey with me and read the first three books, I wanted to put a stake in the ground with this book to say this is where I've come so far in my understanding of God's vision for us. Little did I realize that although I have done exactly that, even this book has taken on a life of its own and pushed me further down the road. As I said, sometimes you get more than you bargain for.

In September 2009, my husband handed me a *New York Times* review of a newly released book authored by Pulitzer Prize-winning authors and husband/wife team, Nicholas Kristof and Sheryl WuDunn. A quick online visit to Amazon.com, a couple of mouse clicks, and in a matter of days I was pouring over *Half the Sky: Turning Oppression into Opportunity for Women Worldwide*. It was a watershed moment for me.

Half the Sky is a disturbing exposé of the world's dark and largely forgotten underbelly where the misery and abuse of women and girls break the scales of human suffering. If you haven't read it already, it belongs on your reading list. Sex trafficking, female genocide, genital mutilation, and honor killings are but a few of the atrocities against millions of women and girls that the book brings to light. These may not be normal topics of polite conversation or suitable bedtime reading, but Kristof and WuDunn fearlessly identify a battlefield of epic proportions that the civilized world needs to engage. Here evil has gained the upper hand and countless souls are trapped, helpless to break free without significant outside help.

Although I was already becoming aware of this global tragedy, the book still shocked me in many ways, including a stubborn thread of hope that ran the full length of the book —a thread I didn't expect to find that surfaced in unbelievable stories of women who have been beaten down but are fighting back and courageously advocating for others. But I am at a total loss for words to describe the feeling that swept over me at the end of the book where, while recognizing that Christian organizations are deployed in this fight, the authors threw down the gauntlet for the rest of the church to step up to the plate. I was jolted to read, "Americans of faith should try as hard to save the lives of African women as the lives of unborn fetuses."[3]

What troubled me most about this open challenge to the church was that Christians are not the loudest voices to sound the alarm, nor are we the most visible at the forefront in addressing this humanitarian crisis. As I wrestled with this question, I recalled that historically, Jesus' followers have been known for their ministries of compassion and justice. In the fourth century, the Roman emperor Julian wrote with amazement that Christians "support not only their poor, but ours as well."[4] In the early centuries Christians were renowned for their active opposition to infanticide. They scoured dung heaps for baby girls who had been thrown out to die, took them home, and raised them as their daughters.

I also remembered stories my mother told me when I was

a little girl. Over a hundred years ago (in 1903, to be exact), an earlier version of *Half the Sky* was published. *Things as They Are: Mission Work in Southern India* was a compilation of letters that a Christian missionary named Amy Wilson-Carmichael wrote to tell her supporters back home about atrocities against women and girls that she was discovering as she visited villages and attempted to evangelize.

In 1895, a young Amy Carmichael arrived in Bangalore (Bengaluru, Karnataka) in southern India for a missionary career that lasted until her death fifty-five years later. As I was growing up, my mother spoke so frequently of this Irish missionary, she almost seemed like a member of our family. I remember my mother's collection of blue books (all written by Amy Carmichael) and the stories she told me of Amy's valiant efforts to rescue little girls whose families were dedicating them to the Hindu temple and of the tragic accident in Amy's sixties, from which she never recovered. Mainly I remember that although Amy Carmichael was already a prolific writer before her accident, she produced other books from her bed of pain that have offered spiritual strength and comfort to countless believers in times of suffering.

When I read *Half the Sky,* I thought of her again — only this time in a different light. Her "rescue" of little girls from dedication to the temple was a daring declaration of war against "marriage to the gods," which was a euphemism for sex trafficking of little girls into a life of temple prostitution. She wasn't writing as a journalist but as a determined *ezer*-warrior[5] in "the smoking hell of battle."[6] The book that chronicled the truth about what was happening is, in her own words, "a battle-book, written from a battle-field where the fighting is not pretty play but stern reality."[7]

Amy received strong opposition from Christian supporters on the home front for her candid (although hardly graphic by today's standards) letters reporting the things happening to little girls and other atrocities, such as honor killings and the abuse of widows. At one point, her supporters contemplated recalling her from the field. She was exasperated and dumb-struck when she was told to edit her reports and to focus on successes instead of upsetting everyone with harsh realities that her supporters did not want to hear. She was unbending to the pressure and prayed instead that her words, "written out of the heat of battle" would be "fire-words." "We are so afraid to offend, so afraid of stark truth, that we write delicately, not honestly. Our smoothness glides over souls. It does not *spur them to action*, even though they be Christians to whom the thought of the glory of the Lord being given to another ought to be unendurable."[8]

Her biographer and friend, Frank Houghton, joined Amy in raising the alarm when, sounding much like Kristof and WuDunn, he wrote, "Christians everywhere in India, men and women of goodwill everywhere ... must care until their own souls are scorched in the fire from which they determine to deliver the little ones."[9]

This book is not like the other books I have written, although *like* those other books, this book is still very much about you, the reader. The work I've done previously has been building a biblical foundation for a better understand-ing of women. This book is the inevitable progression from those earlier books because it moves us from knowledge to action. One can't simply learn the truth and sit on it. Truth not only changes how we see ourselves, it changes what we do and how we live. Those first three books have birthed this one. However, the differences in this book are significant and result largely because of the impact of books like *Things as They Are* and *Half the Sky*.

First, the discussion has widened yet again to include a

new group of female faces who join us from the outer edges of human society, where suffering and oppression are crushing realities from which there is no easy escape. We need these women in this discussion as much as they need us, for if the questions we ask and the answers we embrace do not give them the same hope and kingdom purpose we seek for ourselves, then our conclusions cannot be trusted.

Second, the emphasis is global, so the stories and illustrations are drawn largely from other cultures. We have made many mistakes in drawing conclusions and making assertions from the Bible in isolation from the rest of the world. I cannot alone remedy that problem, and there is much work to be done in this regard. But I can at least raise the issue and make sure that in my work, I am making an effort to engage a global perspective.

Because many of the illustrations point to abuses, it is important to clarify that my intention is *not* to demonize some cultures and exonerate others. Every culture has plusses and minuses, and every culture (including our own) is complicit in atrocities against women. Women and girls are trafficked in America. Our newspapers regularly carry stories of violence and abuse against women and girls, often hidden in plain sight. In the dressing room of a women's clinic in the Florida suburbs, I saw a poster about domestic abuse with tear-off tags across the bottom containing a help-line phone number to slip inside your shoe. It was chilling to see that most of the tags had been torn off by previous patients.

Third, God's vision for his daughters is an implicit call to a full-orbed gospel. Amy Carmichael's ministry embodied that gospel. She intended to devote her life to evangelizing the lost. God expanded her efforts to encompass physical acts of rescue, taking care of scores of babies and little children, and bold efforts to draw government attention to atrocities against little girls—in essence, to be a force for God's justice for the helpless. This shift was not a distraction from the gospel but a centering on its fullness. Whenever anyone argued with her that the gospel was only proclamation and didn't also include acts of mercy and social justice, she was emphatic: "God didn't make you all mouth."[10]

But what takes my breath away is that what looked to supporters and at times even to Amy herself like a detour from her original mission to proclaim the gospel actually turned out to be a brilliantly subversive tactic against the Enemy. For several years, she had tried relentlessly to break through the unyielding iron gates of the Hindu caste system with the gospel. With the help of a seven-year-old girl, God showed her to a side door. A ministry that might have produced only a handful of believers ended up generating hundreds of Christians who still today are rescuing children and spreading the gospel in India.

In my search for answers, one of the outcomes I didn't anticipate was that God's vision for his daughters is taking us somewhere. God's vision for us doesn't just reassure us that we matter and that our lives do count for something. God's vision compels us to look beyond ourselves, to ponder a picture of how things were meant to be that leaves us aching for his will to be done on earth as it is in heaven, and to look for ways to participate in moving the world toward that goal. One of the biggest issues confronting us today is the battle cry of Amy Carmichael and the burning challenge of *Half the Sky*.

Christianity has often been a compassionate force for good in this world. No matter where it occurs—when there is flooding, an earthquake, or a hurricane and thousands are suddenly swept into the clutches of disaster—individual Christians and churches are at the forefront of an outpouring of relief and aid, as well they should be. At home when little ones go missing, hundreds of volunteers are out combing the brush for evidence that may lead to recovery. But we seem to miss the chronic, systemic tragedies that are snatching one anonymous life at a time, even though the casualty count surpasses the losses in all these combined natural calamities—what according to Kristof and WuDunn is "the paramount moral challenge" of the twenty-first century.[11]

I'm not sure of all that has transpired in the intervening years between the publishing of *Things as They Are* and *Half the Sky*, nor do I understand why just now growing numbers of Christian women are feeling greater concern about what is happening to women throughout the world. I only know that as I have searched for answers, God's vision for us and this global crisis have come together, and I can't escape the connection. This crisis is devastating the lives of countless women and girls. Of course this is every Christian's concern—male as well as female. But as women, we have a natural connection with these female sufferers that compels us to speak up on their behalf. As followers of Jesus, we have a strategic responsibility to raise the alarm within the body of Christ and an enormous potential to make a difference

Bishop J. C. Ryle, a nineteenth-century British evangelical, sounds a relevant challenge: "Let the diligence of Christ be an example to all Christians.... Like Him, let us labor to do good in our day and generation, and to leave the world a better world than we found it.... Let us awake to a sense of our individual responsibility."[12]

What started out as a quest to find reassurance that we matter to God, that our identity in him is rock solid, and that our purpose is secure expands in this book to include an overt call to action. That action may take a variety of different forms, but it is inherent to the gospel and to God's calling on his daughters. It is no small matter that women comprise half the church. In many countries women make up a significantly higher percentage of believers—80 percent in China and 90 percent in Japan. In India, during Amy Carmichael's tenure the percentage of Christian females in her expanding ministry was at many points nearly 100 percent. Although everyone is concerned about the need to reach more men, maybe these high percentages of women should make us wonder what God is doing, for he often forges significant inroads for the gospel by beginning with women. Perhaps we ought to be asking what he might do through us. When you stop to think of it, in sheer numbers, the potential we possess for expanding the kingdom of God is staggering.

Sometimes when you're searching for answers, you get more than you bargain for. I hope you get more than you bargained for as you read this book. I hope too that once you see God's earthshaking global vision for you, for the rest of your life you will be unwilling to settle for less.

CHAPTER 1

GOING GLOBAL

"We don't have to have daughters anymore!"[1]

I was appalled. The book I was reading, *Half the Sky*, is a disturbing account of the plight of women and girls in *our* twenty-first-century world. It describes an ongoing humanitarian crisis of staggering proportions and unspeakable suffering—a rampant and brutalizing devaluation of the world's daughters. Barely into the introduction, I was already shaken by what I was learning.

The disturbing words on the page in front of me came from a Chinese man who was exulting over the availability of ultrasound. His cause for joy? The "happy" prospect ultrasound introduces to enable sex-selective abortions. While many Chinese are appalled at such thinking and treasure their daughters, the statement reflects an attitude present in many cultures where sons are held at a premium and the birth of a daughter is a disappointment (at best). Under China's one-child policy, according to this man, technology has delivered the perfect solution. Now Chinese couples who share his perspective can avoid wasting on daughters the one chance their government allows in their desperate quest for sons.

The selective abortion of females—a genocide of epic proportions—is merely the tip of the iceberg that Kristof and

WuDunn have labeled "the paramount moral challenge" of the twenty-first century — "the struggle for gender equality in the developing world."[2] That struggle takes on new meaning when you read brutal accounts of female genocide, the trafficking of young girls, honor killings, bride burnings, female genital mutilation, gang rapes, and forced exposure to AIDS. The list goes on. Equality here boils down to freedoms and opportunities that we in the West simply take for granted — education, basic healthcare, legal protection against assaults, and the right to make decisions for ourselves and lead productive lives.

"Wait a minute," you may be thinking, "I thought this book was about God's global vision for women. Don't the sufferings of women in the world belong in a different book?"

There was a time when I would have thought so, but 9/11 changed all that for me. On the day America's national security was breached we shared a frightening sense of vulnerability that is experienced *routinely* in other regions of the world. Color-coded threat levels, heightened airport security, and occasional alerts of terrorist activity keep that fear alive in us. It was a jarring moment when we were forced to admit that we are not invincible. Our world is broken too. Even on the sunniest of days, suffering and loss can invade without warning and in an instant completely reconfigure the landscape of our lives.

Author Jim Wallis has astutely observed what happened. "On September 11 America joined the world."[3] Our membership was long overdue. Painful as the process has been for us, the benefits of widening our perspective to include the rest of the world are earthshaking, especially the relevance of this development to the conversation we are about to commence concerning God's vision for his daughters.

ENDING ISOLATION

In the aftermath of 9/11 and from the comfort of our own homes, we were confronted by scenes and situations wholly alien to us. Without any effort on our part, the world was expanding right before our eyes. First came scenes of Afghan women encased in sky blue burkas, described by a *Time* reporter as "a kind of body bag for the living."[4] From our Western vantage point, these women floated across our television screens like aliens from a distant planet. We were shocked by accounts of Taliban enforcers whipping Afghan women for revealing their ankles, even when the culprit that caused the exposure was a sudden gust of wind.

This wasn't anything like the casual armchair reading of *National Geographic* articles about another culture in some distant land. Our senses had been jarred awake by the tragedy in our own country. An international curtain had been shredded. Now with heightened sensitivities we were seeing for ourselves how the tragedy that changed our lives was impacting the lives of women elsewhere in the world and joining their stories to ours.

It was as if a dam had suddenly burst as my desire surged to know more about southwestern Asia and the Middle East, and information poured in. For the first time, my reading list included such titles as *Nine Parts of Desire*, *Reading Lolita in Tehran*, *Kite Runner*, *Three Cups of Tea*, and more recently *Half the Sky*. Illuminating conversations followed with individuals from cultures completely foreign to mine. I couldn't (still can't) get enough.

Somewhere in the process of reading and learning I crossed a Rubicon of sorts. No longer could I tell myself my white, middle-class, suburban American world is all that matters. No longer could I close my eyes to these unfamiliar (and sometimes disturbing) realities and convince myself that life as I know it here is, or even ought to be considered, the norm. No longer could I continue my quest to unearth the Bible's message for women in the isolation of the West. I had reached a point of no return that unleashed a flood of changes—two with special relevance to the purpose of this book.

TUNNEL VISION

The first change for me was both sudden and dramatic and targeted my own work. I saw, for the first time, a jaw-dropping connection between the women in the Bible and women of today's Middle East that revolutionized how I study the Bible. Glimpses I was gaining of life in the Middle East and in other patriarchal societies breathed life into Bible characters (women and men), who, since my early childhood, had been trapped inside a two-dimensional flannel graph world. With information I was learning from patriarchal cultures, the stories of women leaped off the pages of my Bible and into my world with an earthshaking potency, depth, and relevance that turned my world upside down.

In hindsight it makes a lot of sense, after all, the Bible isn't an American book. To be honest, the American culture is as far removed from the ancient culture of the Bible as you can get. The message loses its potency and sometimes completely escapes us when read solely through an American lens instead of through the eyes of those who understand the ancient biblical culture.

Unaided by that missing perspective, it is easy to mistake women's stories in the Bible as sidebars to the more significant stories of men. However, when a global perspective is injected, women's stories become far more than inspirational fodder for women's Bible studies and soothing devotional books. Against the backdrop of the ancient patriarchal culture, moments (and Scripture is peppered with them) when a woman steps out to occupy center stage of the biblical narrative are countercultural events, for patriarchy's interest is in men and what the men are achieving. The Bible doesn't maintain that monolithic focus but repeatedly draws women into the action as unflinching heroines of the faith, stalwart kingdom builders, and valiant rescuers of the royal line of Christ. Filled with heart-stopping drama, Job-like wrestlings with God, and accounts of bold courage that changed the world, suddenly these ancient texts link women of a bygone era with women of the twenty-first century with an earthy richness and fresh relevance that raises the bar for what we might do in our day.

Contrary to long-held interpretations, biblical narratives that spotlight women hold their own next to the weighty and impassioned preaching of Old Testament prophets and the rich theological writings of New Testament apostles. Women in the Bible are wise teachers. They offer up a boatload of profound theology intended to enrich the *whole* church's understanding of who God is, what it means to walk with him, and how we are to build his kingdom in this broken world.

I grieved (still do grieve) at how unaware we in the West are of our own cultural blindness—a sort of tunnel vision that plagues us all—and of our feeling of absolute certainty that without leaving our American shores, we are capable of explaining the Bible's message to ourselves, and to the rest of the world as well. I marvel that we could imagine understanding God's message for women without acquainting ourselves with the ancient cultural context through which that message is communicated. What have we been thinking?! And how much has this cost us?

Poking and prodding Greek and Hebrew syntax at a remote distance from the world of the Bible, even digging through archaeological artifacts, systematic theologies, commentaries, and history books (important as these are), can only take us so far. Without engaging residents of those cultures — *actually letting them teach us* — we lack the perspective necessary to unlock (and which we now need to recapture) the teachings of God's Word for women globally. Women in the developing world's patriarchal cultures are brought up with a perspective similar to ancient patriarchal cultures, and they can help us if we will only listen.

The good news is that with globalization, technology, and mounting immigration rates, the rest of the world is coming to us — arriving on our doorstep! Foreigners among us are an indispensible resource that we have historically neglected to our own impoverishment, for we think mainly how *their* lives will change for the better by being with us. This is, however, a two-way street. And for our own sakes as well as for theirs, we need to listen and learn from those who have much to teach us.

No Woman Left Behind

The second major post-9/11 change crept up on me by stealth. When 9/11 cracked open the barrier that for generations divided the West from the rest of the world, not only did it expose the fact that we've been studying God's Word in isolation, it also revealed the fact that our discussion of the Bible's message for women is isolated too.

I only became aware of the extent of this isolation over time. Having twice been excluded from the conversation myself (initially because of singleness and subsequently through infertility), I was painfully aware of the need to expand the circle. Left out for reasons beyond my control and aware of so many other women who for various reasons were also counted out, I was determined to find out if God's message for women was *universal*—encompassing the full spectrum of every woman's life regardless of her demographics or circumstances.

Can we miss or lose or spoil or be cheated of God's purposes for his daughters? Are God's purposes for women only for those whose lives go from early adulthood to "I do" and from there to the delivery room? Or are his purposes dynamic enough to leave no woman or girl behind? Studying with these new broader parameters in place changes the entire discussion and takes it to a deeper level. My questions opened the way for me to explore the bigness of God's heart and purposes for his daughters.

But it wasn't until *Half the Sky* took me to the forgotten fringes of female existence that I began to grasp how far this commitment was leading and that even these questions were too narrow. What if a soul is completely ravaged—brutalized and dehumanized until there is nothing left but an empty shell? Does the gospel only offer such a woman salvation, or does it also establish her as a participant in the Grand Story that God is weaving for the world? Are God's purposes for his daughters indestructible, or do they collapse under the weight of the world's evils?

The plight of women in the world became a tipping point confronting me with millions of shattered women and girls who are forgotten in our quest to understand what God has to say to us and who belong in this conversation. Stories defined by unspeakable brutality, oppression, exploitation, and powerlessness test the limits of the gospel's power to restore wholeness and purpose to women whose lives are living nightmares. *Half the Sky* blew the walls out on my thinking by horrifying me with scenes of an evil malignancy from which I had been shielded. Kristof and WuDunn put faces, stories, and statistics on my definition of "universal" by introducing me to women enduring unspeakable atrocities and injustice — women for whom the gospel message and its redeeming power are intended.

Bringing these women into this discussion changes everything. In our culture, the church has tended to concentrate on a tiny segment of the female population — a narrow, prosperous, protected, well-educated female demographic located in the comfortable midsection of human society. The prosperity we enjoy shapes *both* the questions we ask and the answers we embrace. And we — both the women who are asking and the Christian leaders who are defining the answers — are clueless that this is happening. We can ask questions like, "Do I plan to use my college degree or set it aside?" and "Should I be a stay-at-home mom or work outside the home?" But for the rest of the world, these questions are unimaginable luxuries. For them, education is a lifeline that promises a better life for a woman and her children and will doubtless benefit her community.

Working outside the home is not an option where grinding poverty exists and there are hungry mouths to feed. Everybody works. Our cloistered discussions about God's purposes for women and the resulting infighting that ensues among us leave women elsewhere in the world scratching their heads. Blinded by the insulation of prosperity, we are at risk of transmitting a message as irrelevant and unworkable as Marie Antoinette's solution for the starving masses: "Let them eat cake!" — a message that when sanctioned as "biblical" is cruelly beyond the reach of those with less.

A GLOBAL CONVERSATION

We need a global conversation about the Bible's message for women because a global conversation safeguards us from proclaiming a prosperity gospel for women that works for some (at least for a time) and is utterly crushing to vast numbers of women in our own culture and elsewhere in the world. The Bible's message for women doesn't depend on ideal circumstances, but applies fully to those who live in the brutal outskirts of society where poverty engulfs, education is nonexistent, women's bodies are ravaged, and lives are in constant peril simply because they are female.

Global thinking raises deeper questions and sends us in search of answers that are expansive and dynamic enough to frame every woman's life from birth to death. Within this wider global context, we will discover—for their sakes and for ours—the true strength of God's message for women. Here we will unlock the gospel's potency to bring wholeness and purpose to a trampled and discarded life. This is where we will plumb the depths of God's love for his daughters and see for ourselves that no life is ever beyond the reach of the gospel's restorative powers, no matter how a woman's story plays out. Until we go global, we can never be sure of our questions, much less the answers we affirm.

We need a global conversation because, frankly, the Bible invites that challenge. Every generation faces new issues, crises, and changes. The present generation is no exception. We bear responsibility to test afresh the timelessness of God's Word and its relevance to "today" with current scenarios, possibilities, and issues beyond the experience of previous generations. The bunker is no place for Christians to retreat when some new idea surfaces, major cultural shifts occur, an unanticipated opportunity bursts on the scene, or injustice comes to light. Instead we must fearlessly rise to the challenge.

Our habit of erecting walls of defense to protect ourselves against the cultural shifts and changes that surround us is a denial of Jesus' calling on us to engage the world around us and to join his kingdom-building efforts. For our own sakes and for the sake of our sisters worldwide, we can and must fearlessly test the Bible's message for us to see if it holds up under the worst that the twenty-first century dishes out. Jesus announced his kingdom as "good news to the poor." Let's find out what that good news means for all his daughters.

We need a global conversation because the Bible itself is global. God's Word has never been the exclusive property of the elite. God's Word is for the world. If anything, the Bible gives priority to the weak, the oppressed, and the poor and is tougher on privileged people who hold the reins of wealth and power but refuse to wield their advantages for the good of others. Jesus had little tolerance for self-centered individuals who indulged themselves and hoarded the comforts of this earthly life. His heart was with the suffering and oppressed, and we can be sure the Bible's message reflects the same commitment.

Scanning the twenty-first-century horizon will help us move our discussion about women into the global arena by giving us some sense of the scope of the challenge before us.

THE TWENTY-FIRST-CENTURY LANDSCAPE FOR WOMEN

The landscape for women in the twenty-first century is a polarized world of extremes that, to be honest, is confusing to women. At one end of the spectrum, women have broken through the glass ceiling to secure posts of leadership, power, and achievement that rival their male counterparts. Women have arrived and in growing numbers are succeeding in the highest echelons of government, business, religion, education, sports, and the entertainment industry. It is a new day for women. Those who enjoy the benefits of education, wealth, and freedom are blessed with a lavish smorgasbord of exciting options. Parents today are telling their daughters, "You can be anything you want to be."

At the same time and in the same world, a Chinese man rejoices that "we don't have to have daughters anymore." Dreams may come true where prosperity abounds, but the world is a sinister, frighteningly unsafe, degrading place for millions of daughters who are powerless to stop what is happening to them. Honor killings, sex trafficking, child marriages, female infanticide, and stranded and impoverished widows are not yesterday's news. They are happening at this very moment to catastrophic numbers of women — wildly beyond epidemic levels. It is simply mind numbing.

Imagine, if you can, the reality represented by the following statements. "It appears that more girls have been killed in the last fifty years, precisely because they were girls, than men were killed in all the wars of the twentieth century. More girls are killed in this routine 'gendercide' in any one decade than people were slaughtered in all the genocides of the twentieth century."[5] Research indicates that worldwide around *three million* women and girls have been kidnapped or sold (sometimes by their own families) into the sex trade, which in effect means they are "the property of another person and in many cases could be killed by their owner with impunity."[6] Put more concretely, "far more women and girls are shipped into brothels each year in the early twenty-first century than African slaves were shipped into slave plantations each year in the eighteenth or nineteenth centuries."[7]

During the 2008 U.S. presidential election, two stories ran concurrently in the press that revealed a striking contrast between the extremes experienced by twenty-first-century women. The media was trumpeting then New York Senator Hillary Clinton's near capture of the Democratic Party's nomination for the presidency, bringing a woman within reach of the most powerful office in the world. It was a moment to savor. Yet while crowds were cheering and voters were turning out in record numbers in support of Hillary's historic race for the White House, reports of brutal honor killings in Islamabad surfaced on the Internet. Three Afghan teenage girls were buried alive for the crime of merely planning to choose their own husbands. Two older women, a mother and an aunt, were shot to death while pleading desperately for the girls' lives to be spared. And who were their executioners? The girls' fathers, brothers, and uncles.

THE CHALLENGE TO THE CHURCH

Into this world of breathtaking opportunities and shocking atrocities, the church attempts to speak a solid message for women. But the message we offer is not robust enough to address the opportunities, changes, and extremities of life in a fallen world. It is too small for successful women leaders in the secular world and too weak to restore full meaning and purpose to women who have been trampled. It is not far-reaching enough to encompass every woman's whole life or the variegations that exist for us within this multicultural, rapidly changing world.

Instead of addressing the wide range of questions and situations women are facing today, we focus mainly on marriage and motherhood, and that within a two-parent, single-income family. We overlook all the other seasons of a woman's life—which impacts every girl and adult woman and excludes entirely women whose lives follow a different path. Our message has taken on a negative, defensive tone and doesn't capitalize on the positive, life-affirming, kingdom nature of God's message for women.

The twenty-first century poses a threefold challenge to the church. *First, what message does the church offer women in the twenty-first century?* Women are looking for a message large enough to encompass every woman's life and strong enough to empower us to fight the battles God has placed in our paths. The world needs a gospel vision of relationships between men and women. Will the Bible deliver?

Second, what will the church do to address the rampant suffering of women throughout our world? Will we lag behind the rest of the world in fostering the flourishing of women and girls, or will we join together in taking the lead in global advocacy and activism on behalf of the widow, the trafficked, the marginalized, and oppressed? Jesus and the Old Testament prophets call us to this.

Third, what message are we sending to the world by how we value and mobilize our own daughters? Will the whole church openly benefit from women's gifts and contributions, or will the body of Christ attempt to fulfill a mission that dwarfs our resources without the full participation of half the church? What is it costing us when half the church's gifts go untapped?

The Chinese proverb that "women hold up half the sky" is a fitting reminder that women are one of the world's most precious natural resources. Kristof and WuDunn assert, "Women aren't the problem, but the solution,"[8] for when women are educated and empowered to contribute, they are good for communities, children, education, health, and economies. These authors' research provides names, faces, and stories of Heroic (with a capital "H") women who rise up from the ashen ruins of their own lives to combat the evil that has ravaged them and to fight to make a different world for others.

Women do hold up half the sky.

I have successfully finished reading the book—mostly at an altitude of 37,000 feet en route to speaking engagements and stopping repeatedly to pull myself together in order to keep reading. Having finished, however, I'm finding that the book isn't finished with me.

As I write, the numbers mount. Another life snuffed out or thrown out to die. Another little girl sold off and bludgeoned or drugged into serving brothel clients ... with a smile and almost certainly contracting AIDS. Another woman dying in childbirth for lack of basic medical care. This crisis isn't old history. It is happening now!

The twenty-first century is a time of unprecedented opportunity for the church to be a beacon of hope for women throughout the world. This is a moment for us to put on display before a watching world the greatness and beauty of the gospel of Jesus Christ and the radical difference he makes in relationships between men and women as we serve him together. This is a time for us to value and foster the flourishing of women and girls and to join together in leading in global advocacy and activism on behalf of the widow, the trafficked, the marginalized, and oppressed. Blessings from God carry responsibility for others.

The opportunity is not ours alone. The strongest voices speaking into women's lives in the twenty-first century are Islam and feminism—systems that reside at opposite ends of the spectrum. Does the church's message for women stake out the middle ground, or does the gospel lead the way to something much better? After years of asking questions and digging into Scripture in search of answers, I am convinced we have a message for women that is ready to take on the challenges of the new millennium—a message that far outstrips these other voices and unlocks the untapped potential of half the church. And what may surprise a lot of readers is the fact that this message is good news for our brothers too. This book sets out to unpack that message—directly, clearly, and from a global perspective—so that no woman or girl is ever left behind.

DISCUSSION QUESTIONS

1. Describe ways in which women's lives in this country have changed over the past century. How have these changes benefitted you?

2. How would your life be different if you had been born in a culture where women are generally not valued and the birth of a daughter is a disappointment?

3. What challenges do we as Christians face in speaking into women's lives with a message that equips them to live in a world where we are not all the same?

4. How do those challenges become more difficult if a young woman who has been rescued from sex trafficking joins the conversation? Why is it essential that we include her?

5. Why can we fearlessly ask today's questions of God's Word, and why is it important to you personally that we do so?

CHAPTER 2

IDENTITY THEFT

Raising a daughter is like watering your neighbour's garden.
—Hindu saying

Tamam was Palestinian, but she might as well have been Hindu. She grew up in northern Israel, in the ancient city of Akko, located in Western Galilee. She and her family were among 156,000 Palestinians who remained in Israel during the 1948 Arab-Israeli War. Journalist Geraldine Brooks tells Tamam's story in *Nine Parts of Desire*: "She was the last of five daughters; her name, which translates as 'enough,' or 'finished,' was her parents plea for an end to the long run of unwanted girls. Their prayer was answered, several years later, with the birth of two sons."[1] Historically and even today in patriarchal cultures, a daughter has far less value than a son. In those cultures, sons build a father's name, estate, and stature in the community. A daughter, however, will one day leave to build another man's house or, euphemistically, to water the neighbor's garden.

A friend of mine relayed a similar story of a Jordanian father living in the West and married to a North American, who (contrary to his culture) was delighted at the births of his first three children—all girls. However, after each birth it took him days to muster up the courage to phone home and tell his parents. When his wife finally gave birth to a son, he grabbed the phone immediately and dialed Jordan. His mother made a high-pitched trilling noise to celebrate the news.

Kristof and WuDunn report something far more sinister than disappointment at the birth of a daughter—*female infanticide*. Fathers killing their daughters for not being sons. Mothers killing their daughters because their husbands threaten to divorce them if they keep their infant daughters.[2] Even for baby girls who survive that first brush with death, mortality rates are sky high since little girls often don't receive the same nutrition or medical care as their brothers. "All told, girls in India from one to five years of age are 50 percent more likely to die than boys the same age. The best estimate is that a little Indian girl dies from discrimination every four minutes."[3]

The husband isn't always the only one to pressure his wife for male progeny. His family can exert unbearable pressure and may even exact punishment if she fails. A woman in Pakistan poisoned her infant daughter "after her father-in-law beat her for giving birth to a girl."[4] The findings of Kristof and WuDunn are chilling: "Sometimes women in Pakistan or China kill their newborn daughters simply because daughters are less prestigious than sons."[5] One woman drowned her baby daughter "because girls are unlucky."[6]

Then there is Marika. Her story takes the discussion of how the world values daughters to an all-time low. It would be disturbing enough to say she is an isolated case. If only that were so! But Marika's story is repeated over and over again today until, when the tally of Marikas soared into the millions, statisticians simply lost count.

The promise of a waitressing job in Tel Aviv was the bait

that lured this well-meaning but desperate nineteen-year-old Ukrainian into the brutal world of sex trafficking. With a sick mother, an unemployed alcoholic father, and two younger sisters to support, Marika saw this job offer as a way to help her family survive. It was a hoax of unimaginable consequences. Instead of working as a waitress, Marika became helplessly ensnared by powerful and brutal sex traffickers, held hostage to their demands and forced into prostitution.

What kept Marika sane throughout her nightmarish ordeal was remembering who she is. Male clients called all the girls "Natasha." She wasn't Natasha. She was Marika.

> At first I thought it strange being called by another name. But very soon I came to accept it as my escape. When I was alone in my thoughts and my dreams, I was Marika—free from this prison. But when I went with a man, I became this other woman—this prostitute called Natasha, who was cold and dead inside me. Natasha was my nightmare. Marika was my salvation. I never told any of these men my real name. And they never asked.[7]

The world is regularly making negative value statements about women and girls. We may respond with disbelief to horrifying stories like Marika's without recognizing the equally appalling message being transmitted to the world's daughters when baby girls can be lightly discarded or neglected, women are abused with impunity, and wives can be cast out on the street if they don't produce sons or are widowed. Even in the "land of the free," where education and prosperity have vastly improved the terrain for women, our value and identities are at risk so long as they are derived from something or someone we can lose.

The Tamams and Marikas of this world draw a circle that is large enough to encompass every woman's story. Tamam was unwanted. Every mention of her name is a reminder of that painful fact. Marika "lives" in a hell on earth where choice no longer exists and all she can do to keep her soul alive is to cling desperately to fading memories of the girl she used to be. What does it do to a girl to be called "Enough"? What happens to Marika if she hears "Natasha" one too many times?

A Golden Opportunity

This is a moment of unprecedented opportunity for the church. This is a moment to speak into this void with a positive, affirming gospel message for a global audience of women who are searching for hope. This is a moment for believers to embody a gospel culture where *both* halves of the church are thriving because following Jesus produces a climate of honor, value, and love and we are serving God together as he intended from the beginning. This is a golden opportunity to restore to women the indestructible and elevated identity that they have inherited as God's daughters and that a fallen world has stolen from them.

Yet instead of casting a powerful gospel vision that both validates and mobilizes women, the church's message for women is mixed at best—guarded, negative, and small at worst. Everywhere we go, a line has been drawn establishing parameters for how much or how little we are permitted to do within the church. As in the wider culture, there are always exceptions—a tiny minority of women who manage to live beyond the parameters drawn for their sisters. But culture shock awaits many women who migrate from the academy or the secular workplace to the church. In the former, opportunities are vast and their contributions valued and pursued. In the church, what they have to offer often goes unnoticed or is restricted to "appropriate" zones within the church. Warnings about the "feminization of the church" communicate a clear message that there is "enough" of us and what the church really needs is more sons. I must admit my heart sank when a team of women ministering in Africa told me that women who had converted from Islam to Christianity were "disappointed" that the gospel didn't offer them more.

Does the gospel only offer a guarded, small message for women? Or does the gospel overturn the culture's small, diminishing, and often degrading message for women with a clarion call to live within the boundless parameters Jesus defines—to "love the Lord your God with *all* your heart, *all* your soul, *all* your mind, and *all* your strength" (Mark 12:30, emphasis added)?

Who tells us who we are? Who alone has the right to define our worth? Are we at the mercy of gender, culture, circumstances, and fear? Or is there a Voice that trumps all others to give us an indestructible identity and rich, durable kingdom purposes for our lives?

AGAINST THE TIDE

The first statement about women in the Bible differs sharply with these scenarios. No other view of women *begins* to compare. It's hard to imagine a stronger indictment of the way women and girls are devalued, discarded, objectified, trafficked, silenced, marginalized, and in any other manner degraded or diminished. It's hard to imagine a more powerful statement of the enormous value God places on his daughters or a grander vision for our lives. Never has there been a more ringing endorsement of the *strategic necessity* of the gifts and contributions half the church has to offer. And the statement that does all this comes straight from the mouth of God:

Then God said, "Let us make [human beings] in our image, in our likeness." ... So God created [human beings] in his own image, in the image of God he created [them]; male *and female* he created them (Genesis 1:26–27, emphasis added).

Page one of the Bible shatters every negative value statement the world has ever made about women by offering up the most exalted view of women anyone could imagine. God's story begins by emphatically corroborating the view that "women hold up half the sky," but takes this statement much, much further when God names women, along with men, as his *image bearers*.

Furthermore, God's first word about women completely shatters the notion that boys are more valuable than girls. God isn't calling men and asking women to hang back. He gives *both* male and female the exact same identity—to be his image bearers. He gives *both* the exact same responsibilities when he entrusts all of creation to his image bearers, calling them to be fruitful and multiply and to rule and subdue the whole earth (Genesis 1:26, 28). Words spoken here encompass every human being, every facet of human life, and every square inch of earth, and leave every other conceivable view of women (or of men) in the dust.

MISSING THE POINT

The creation narrative is one of those landmine sections of the Bible that we've been walking over for years, never realizing our feet have come within inches of tripping an explosive, life-transforming truth that catapults the Bible's message for women into the stratosphere. This is where God's story for the world begins. He is vision-casting—launching the most ambitious enterprise the world has ever known and defining who we are and what our mission will be. God is setting the stage for the drama about to play out, casting all humanity in leading roles, and unveiling his kingdom vision—his strategic plan, if you will—for the world.

If we are to understand who we are as women, the rest of Scripture must be understood in light of the vision God is casting here. Our calling as image bearers shapes how we see ourselves and is the lens through which we are to understand our mission in the world and to read every other passage of Scripture that addresses us as women and as believers.

To be sure, we lost sight of God's grand vision in the fall. We live in the broken ruins of that beautiful but forgotten world God originally created. But God has never given up on his original dream. No matter how bad things get or how broken and hopeless the world seems to be, God's vision is still the game plan. He has not left us to feel our way blindly through the darkness. We have the creation story, where God spells out his vision. The first two chapters of Genesis contain the clues to God's original vision and are the passages we must relentlessly probe for answers. Jesus came to reconnect us to our Creator and put us back on mission. This is where Jesus is taking us.

Yet, instead of bringing our toughest, global, real-life questions to the text, the very tools that will help detonate our small ideas of ourselves and of God's vision for us, we have turned this Genesis passage into a stockpile of ammunition for a variety of debates and a catalog of reasons that distinguish human beings from the rest of creation. We gather arguments against folks who believe in evolution. We search for fodder for one side or the other in the controversy over whether God actually created the world in literal twenty-four-hour days. We bog down in wranglings over what equality between men and women really means and what, if any, are our respective roles. God is revealing the greatness of his heart for us and delivering stunning, life-transforming news about ourselves and our mission in this world, and too often we are missing the point.

Part of the problem, if I may be so bold, comes from how professional theologians and biblical scholars talk about what it means to be God's image bearers. Don't get me wrong; I love reading theology books and biblical commentaries and would be hindered in my work without them. But I confess I am often disappointed with what they have to say on this subject. Instead of giving us an expansive, jaw-dropping view of God's ambitious plans for us, the focus narrows to a technical discussion as theologians try to pinpoint specific ways in which human beings resemble God.

Next to nothing, really, is said to make us feel the weight—the significance—of the mission God is entrusting to humanity or the challenge embedded in his decision to make us his image bearers. The assumption is that the commands to "be fruitful and multiply, and fill the earth" (NASB) are restricted to physical reproduction. Nothing startling about that. Ruling and subduing remind us of our noble calling to care for all creation, but somehow we remain unphased. We aren't rocked by a radically different view of ourselves or our world. We aren't put on alert because God has delegated to us—to all of us—a profound responsibility for what is happening all around us and for the care and wise stewardship of all creation.

Instead, we end up with a list of bullet points—an inventory of God's *communicable* attributes, those qualities belonging to God that he shares with us. Moral, spiritual, intellectual, and relational qualities make the list. What ultimately happens is that instead of being shaken by a visionary calling that will take everything we have to offer and more, we end up with a *static* list of attributes that are echoes of the divine in us. Efforts to pin down the precise meaning of image bearer (which the text does not do) ultimately box up the subject. We are sitting on the launch pad of God's vision for the world talking about nuts and bolts and heat-resistant tiles instead of buckling up for the ride of our lives. As a result, we brush right past some of the most important statements in the Bible and miss the breathtaking vista God is spreading before his daughters and his sons.

It is a classic example of missing the forest for the trees.

When God created human beings in his "image" and "likeness," he was designating us as his representatives on the earth. Instead of running things directly himself, he chose us as his intermediaries to run things here in this world. As his image bearers, we speak and act on his behalf. This is not only about Christians. Every human being is God's image bearer—granted the highest possible rank of all of God's creation. Every human being has a strategic role in God's purposes for the world. Every human being possesses a derived significance—grounded in God himself. And every human being is summoned to the highest of all possible aspirations—not to be God, but *"to be like"* God himself. God is the standard for who we are and what our mission is in this world. By pursuing this loftiest of all goals, we move toward true flourishing as human beings.

Unless and until we probe deeper, there will be no explosive discovery, no blinding burst of light to illumine our path, no vision to capture our imaginations. There will be no booming Voice to trump the negative messages we're hearing and no exalted calling that compels us to embody the gospel in our relationships and work. We won't be telling women like Tamam and Marika that their God-given identity is secure and can't be destroyed, that the way they are regarded and trampled is a personal offense to God because they bear his image, that they have leading roles in his story and nothing can keep them out. Instead, we walk away yawning as though nothing all that important is happening here—unimpressed with the glorious identity God just dropped in our laps. Given the fact that we've just heard one of the most startling announcements in all of history, it is remarkable that we do so little with this and must be somewhat disappointing to God that he doesn't get more of a reaction out of us.

A ROYAL REACTION

King David reacted. He kept digging, and the explosion he triggered threw him to his knees. He was looking at God's statement from the vantage point of a king—the top rung of the human ladder, the pinnacle of human achievement, power, and prestige. From such a lofty position, David didn't suffer from low self-esteem. Yet, what surprised the king as he pondered his image bearer status from a kingly elevation was that his opinion of himself was actually too low. So earthshaking was this discovery and the language he used to describe it is so over the top that many biblical translators have been reluctant to give us the straight translation. Most, but not all: "Yet you have made them [human beings] *a little lower than God* [*Elohim*], and crowned them with glory and honor" (Psalm 8:5 NRSV, emphasis added).

David was dumbfounded. It would hardly have impressed him that being human made him superior to plants and animals. He was already superior in rank to the entire nation of Israel. What did impress David, however, was his rank compared to God. From the altitude of a monarch, he measured the distance God had chosen to establish between himself and human beings. In a state of incredulity the king penned the remarkable statement that we are *"a little lower than God."*

So if we miss the point the first time we encounter it in Genesis, David brings it up again in the Psalms. His words underscore the fact that the world is wide of the mark when it devalues and discards women and girls. By making us "a little lower" than himself, God affixed the highest possible value on his daughters and his sons. It also certainly means (and the church should surely trumpet this) that the Bible's high view of women cannot be surpassed. Our tendency is to look sideways—to compare ourselves and compete with other people. The Bible calls us to raise our eyes and our aspirations and strive to be like God.

Our identity as God's image bearers casts in cement a fundamental equality, dignity, and purpose among all human beings—truth that if embraced and acted on would make the world a better place. But this is just *hors d'oeuvres.* For God isn't just giving us existence, exceedingly high rank, and the whole world too, which in itself is a lot to absorb. He is giving us himself!

OPEN DOOR POLICY

In the early years of Barak Obama's presidency, the nation became obsessed with stories of smartly dressed, impressive-looking people who managed (uninvited, mind you) to gain entry to invitation-only, top-security presidential events. In 2009, decked out in a tuxedo and an elegant red sari, Tareq and Michaele Salahi were gatecrashers at the first state dinner the newly elected President and Mrs. Obama hosted in honor of India's Prime Minister. The interloping pair breezed through metal detectors, the guest list checkpoint, a detail of Marine guards, and the Secret Service (pausing briefly to pose for photographers) to get near the President and First Lady. Later a media uproar ensued when photos surfaced of the Salihis shaking hands with President Obama and smiling like old friends with Vice President Biden. Sipping cocktails, chatting comfortably with dignitaries, politicians, and celebrity guests — these people weren't supposed to get in the door.

If God had wanted, he could have chosen to operate behind a ring of tight security, beyond the reach of human beings who, given that scenario, would no doubt be clamoring to get in. Unlike the occasional cracks a gatecrasher might find in Secret Service coverage, no one would be able to figure out how to break through God's security system by outsmarting a guard or climbing through a window, like the man who got into Queen Elizabeth's bedroom while she was sleeping. We could rattle the gates as long as we liked, but until they opened from the inside, we would be out in the cold without a prayer of getting anywhere near God. Most royals and political leaders do things that way. Access for ordinary citizens is by invitation only, no matter how badly they want in.

This reality makes it all the more remarkable that the God of all creation begins his story by announcing his intention to maintain an open door policy when it comes to us. Before a single human being set foot on this planet, God had already flung the door wide open, issued an official invitation, and put the welcome mat out. Instead of banging on the gates outside, we are invited in, not for a formal handshake and a photo op, but for an ever-deepening, one-on-one relationship with God.

And here's what we so often miss. By naming us as his image bearers, God has made a relationship with himself the strategic center of his purpose for humanity and for the world. Knowing God is as vital to us as the air we breathe — not just a "come to faith" knowing, but the ongoing knowing and endless discoveries of a relationship. Not a destination or a terminus, but an endless quest to know and understand the God who created us. Maneuvering through life without knowing him is as much to our undoing as for an astronaut to attempt a tethered space walk without the oxygen-supply line that connects her to the spacecraft. The image bearer's relationship with God is our north star, the reference point from which we begin to understand everything else—including ourselves.

A million benefits and challenges radiate out from this divine center into our everyday lives. It places us at the center of what God is doing in the world—not as spectators, but as kingdom agents and as leaders with responsibility for what is happening around us. Like the Secretary of State or other members of the President's cabinet, we have derived, but undeniable significance because of the One we represent. Suddenly our mundane and often behind-the-scenes lives are invested with cosmic significance, for we are God's eyes and ears, his hands and feet, his voice in this world. He didn't just level the playing field between men and women; he raised the bar sky high for both sexes, for he wants his image bearers to aspire, to push ourselves, and to reach toward the high calling he has entrusted to us.

"The image of God is a reality toward which we are moving. It is what we are en route to becoming."[8] When you think about it, God's call for us to reflect his image in the world is exhilarating, but it leaves us wondering how to move forward. How does anyone take up such a task? Sometimes help comes from surprising unexpected sources.

IMAGE BEARING 101

One of the best examples of image bearing I've seen came from British actress Helen Mirren. In 2007, the Academy of Motion Pictures awarded Mirren the Oscar for Best Actress for her realistic portrayal of Queen Elizabeth II in *The Queen*. As image bearers go, Mirren is something of an expert. Her portrayal of the British monarch is so masterful, so convincing, it's easy to forget you're watching a performance and to start believing you're seeing the real queen.

One of the riskiest roles for an actor is to portray a famous person everybody knows. Audiences can be critical, especially when they can compare a performance with a living original. Dame Mirren came to this role with two distinct advantages: first, she is an unusually gifted actress, and second, she is British. She grew up watching the Queen. But coasting on both of these advantages would never have been enough to pull off an Oscar-winning performance. She knew she had to work. "The queen was like Big Ben in London," she explained in her posh British accent. "You know, the clock. Always there. You drive by. 'Oh there's Big Ben.' But you don't really look at it. And it's incredibly familiar, but you haven't ever really studied it. And *now* I had to study the queen—psychologically, historically —just try and find as much information as I could about her."[9]

Without direct access to Her Majesty, Mirren depended on video clips, audio recordings, history books, and a keen eye. She scrutinized every detail about the Queen and then she practiced what she saw.

> I studied a great deal of film just to watch her: the way she walks, the way she holds her head, what she does with her hands, exactly where the handbag is held. When she wears her glasses and when she doesn't wear her glasses, which is quite interesting. When there's a tension and when there's a relaxation. Obviously, the physicality was very important.[10]

Evidently, one of the hardest parts was mastering the queen's unique gait. Mirren was undeterred. Again and again she tried and failed until one day, talking with a neighbor in her front garden and pacing back and forth, she finally got it.

The God of justice, goodness, righteousness, and beauty created a world that is perfectly designed to reflect who he is.

> The heavens declare the glory of God.
>> The skies display his marvelous craftsmanship.
> Day after day they continue to speak;
>> night after night they make him known.
> They speak without a sound or a word;
>> their voice is never heard.
> Yet their message has gone throughout the earth,
>> and their words to all the world. (Psalm 19:1–4)

But the place God longs to see the clearest, fullest reflection of himself is in us. The starting place for every daughter is to follow Mirren's example by making God our study—no longer driving past him, like a familiar Big Ben we've gotten used to having around. Instead, with a keen eye to take in every detail, we are to focus on who he is, see the world through his eyes, love what he loves, grieve what he hates, and join his cause.

Helen Mirren's job was to know a very private queen who remains secluded behind palace gates and royal guards. God doesn't barricade himself behind gates or guards, for he wants this more than we do. He invites us in. He reveals himself through the stories of men and women in Scripture. Most of all he gave us Jesus, who as God's perfect image bearer[11] embodies for us exactly what God had in mind when he created us to be his image bearers. Jesus came to reconnect a lost humanity with the God who created us and to put us back on mission as his representatives in the world.

The Bible is peppered with image-bearer language, constantly lifting our eyes to the exalted calling God bestowed on us in the beginning by turning our focus on Jesus. Jesus not only shows us who we were created to be and bridges the gap between ourselves and God, he redefines our terminology. Terms like *love*, *forgive*, and *oneness* take on a more intense and far more costly meaning when they are tied to how Jesus himself embodied them.

- Love each other. Just *as I have loved you*, you should love each other.

- You must be holy *because I am holy.*

- Be kind to each other, tenderhearted, forgiving one another, *just as God through Christ has forgiven you.*

- Your attitude should be *the same attitude that Christ Jesus had.*

- Instead, there must be a spirited renewal of your thoughts and attitudes. You must display a new nature because you are a new person, *created in God's likeness* — righteous, holy, and true.[12]

RE-ENVISIONING DAUGHTERS

The world is wide of the mark when it discards, tramples, and marginalizes God's daughters. Such actions are a personal affront to God himself, for his daughters bear his image. God does not view them as losing investments who one day will water someone else's garden. He commissions His daughters along with his sons to rule and subdue his garden. And, as if to make sure no one misses the point, none other than the apostle Paul himself underscores the radical implications of Jesus' gospel for daughters. I am jolted as I read a letter from Paul to a mixed first-century audience — a group of believers that included women whose births were disappointments to their fathers. What sounds at first to my Western ears like an attempt to exclude women is exactly the opposite. In one brief sentence Paul overthrows cultural bias by raising women to the same status as their brothers: "You are *all sons* of God through faith in Christ Jesus" (Galatians 3:26, emphasis added). In Western, more egalitarian societies, biblical scholars have sometimes amended the translation to read, "You are all *children* of God" (emphasis added) so that women readers won't feel left out. But these modern translations miss the point. One might say raising daughters who are as valued as sons is like watering your own garden.

None of God's daughters will ever bear the name "Enough." He gives us something much more solid and secure to hold us in this broken world than fading memories of "Marika." We are his image bearers—welcomed into the inner circle to know the God who created the universe. We represent him in this world—speaking and acting on his behalf. He is counting on his daughters along with his sons to be guardians of the whole earth and to rule it as he himself would.

This only scratches the surface of the Bible's powerful message for women—a message that applies to every woman and girl who has ever graced this planet. It steels us against the forces of evil in this world. It also awakens us to the awful responsibility we bear, so long as there are Tamams and Natashas in this world. You can't study God for long without realizing that the women we've been discussing are blinking lights on his radar. Following Jesus' example, today's image bearers—*both* halves of the church—have kingdom work to do on their behalf.

In future chapters, we will unpack more good news for God's daughters from this creation narrative. But before we do, we have another matter to address, for trouble looms on the horizon. Our calling is clear, but the path ahead isn't smooth and makes it difficult for us to move forward. Conflict is everywhere. Will conflict in our lives prevent us from making progress, or will it spur us on our way to becoming the image bearers God created us to be?

DISCUSSION QUESTIONS

1. If someone were introducing you to people you were meeting for the first time, what should they say to communicate accurately who you are?

2. What people, relationships, abilities, and achievements form the basis of your identity? Is there any part of your identity that you could lose or already have lost? Explain.

3. How does it change everything for your identity to be grounded in God as his image bearer, and how does this identity speak hope and purpose into every woman's life?

4. What privileges and blessings are yours to enjoy as God's image bearer?

5. What effort does God long to see you make as you cultivate your calling as his image bearer?

CHAPTER 3

BEARING GOD'S IMAGE
IN A BROKEN WORLD

The world is a mess.

I was surfing the Internet searching for data on sex trafficking when I stumbled across a web video entitled "The Girl Effect," from the humanitarian organization Care International.[1] The video opens by flashing this dismal news bulletin across the screen. We already know the world is a mess at one level, but I suspect we are mostly unaware of what this means for women worldwide. What follows in the video is a litany of evidence intended to silence anyone who dares to doubt that somber assessment. Poverty, AIDS, hunger, and war head the list. Visit the websites of any number of other humanitarian organizations, both Christian and secular (World Vision, International Justice Mission, The Bill and Melinda Gates Foundation) and you will find they have a profound understanding that the world is indeed a mess. Nowhere is this more painfully evident than among women worldwide. A stark look at what is happening to women in our world is a jarring reminder that the fall is worse than we ever thought.

This depressing truth for women was again confirmed for me some time later. I was driving home in my car after running errands and listening to NPR's *All Things Considered* when I was blindsided by a graphic report by Ofeibea

Quist-Arcton, a journalist from Ghana. "Mess" doesn't come close to describing what I heard. Her report contained disturbing interviews with women who were victims of sexual violence in the West African nation of Guinea — an outbreak of unspeakable brutality against women. Violence erupted during a military crackdown on a prodemocracy rally in September 2009. The worst of it occurred when, in broad daylight, government troops viciously gang-raped many of the women attending the rally.[2] I will spare you the details.

The nightmare was only beginning for many of the women who were assaulted, and they knew it. The peril they faced next would come from their families, forcing them to conceal (as best they could) the physical and psychological injuries they had suffered. In cultures where a woman's purity is an icon of family honor, rape victims often face double victimization when husbands and relatives reject and punish them for bringing shame on the family. Details in the interviews were so brutal and the victim's accounts so gut-wrenching, I pulled over to the side of the road and wept.

It is one thing to live as God's image bearers in the beautiful garden of Eden where peace and harmony reign and God is your nearest neighbor. It is quite another to live as God's image bearers in a fallen world where women are gang-raped in broad daylight and God is mysteriously absent. What does it mean to bear God's image here ... in the mess where the fall is much worse than we ever imagined?

REALITY CHECK

I would love to live in a perfect world, but I don't. All too often my culture feeds the illusion that perfection is within my grasp. Even the church contributes to the myth and seems to suggest that dreams really do come true. If you follow the formula for right Christian living, we are told, you too can have the perfect marriage, perfect children, perfect health, the perfect home, the perfect career, and plenty of money. A conflict-free life awaits the faithful follower of Jesus. This myth is more widespread and much closer to home than most of us are willing to admit. Sometimes it is difficult to distinguish Cinderella's Magic Kingdom from the kingdom of God.

Although I wouldn't categorize New Testament apostles as pessimists, they don't confuse the real world with fantasy. "Don't be surprised" when bad things happen *to you*,[3] writes Peter. Paul is forthright in admitting he battles a "thorn in [his] flesh,"[4] which isn't going away despite impassioned prayer, faithful living, and a God with the power to remove it. These words reflect the realities we experience but wish to deny: that we and our world are broken, that this side of eternity we will drink deeply of that brokenness, and there will be thorns we can't shake off that accompany us to our graves. The world is a mess and so are we. But *this* is the context in which God is calling his image bearers to kingdom living.

The apostles may shatter our illusion of an Edenic life, but they do not destroy our hope. To the contrary, they are remarkably hopeful, asserting a steady confidence that despite the fallenness that engulfs us, in some mysterious way God still has the upper hand. He will not allow the forces of evil — strong though they may be — to defeat him or derail his kingdom purposes. Followers of Jesus operate under the counterintuitive belief that conflict brought on by the Enemy will ultimately backfire, for conflict actually shapes God's image bearers and fortifies us for the kingdom work we were born to do.

The challenge for us is not to insulate ourselves from conflict (which we ultimately can't do anyway) or to accept it fatalistically, but rather to lean into the conflict — to face it head-on and to engage it. We must ask the hard questions about God, about ourselves, about the state of things in our world, about the meaning of hope and joy and purpose. But we must also respond to what conflict asks of us.

LIVING IN THE CONFLICT

My daughter once had an assignment in her high school literature class to add a chapter to a book they had just read — South African author Alan Paton's *Cry, the Beloved Country*. She wrote a deeply moving chapter of a convicted murderer's tender letter to his grief-stricken mother — a piece of the story that was truly missing.

If I could add another chapter to the Bible, it would come between Genesis 2 and 3 — between creation and the fall. The tragic part about the beautiful Story God is launching at creation is that before the Story ever gets off the ground, conflict rears its ugly head. Three chapters into God's Story, apparently just after God finishes up his final inspection of the work he has done, the whole thing falls apart. There's no deafening firing of rocket engines. No lift-off. No blazing launch that lights up the skies. No chance for us to see, if ever so briefly, what unfallen image-bearer living looks like. There is no opportunity to observe how together Adam and Eve tackle their God-given mandate to be fruitful and multiply and to rule and subdue.

Literary experts tell us every good story has conflict. Stories that grip us most (at least in novels and movies) are those with nail-biting conflict that puts us on the edge of our seats, wondering how it will all turn out. Conflict — which happens when some person or force opposes the protagonist and threatens them and/or something they value deeply — actually *makes* the story. In fact, *without conflict a story has no plot.*

God's Story is thick with plot. You can't get through three chapters before the deadliest conflict breaks out. Like an enormous wrecking ball, conflict blasts through everything God has put in place. From Genesis 3 on, conflict rains down (literally in some places)—throughout the Bible and straight into our lives. And we are left in the smoldering ruins of that once-beautiful and perfect world to figure out how to make our way forward without drowning in the conflict.

MISSING PLOT?

To be honest, I've never thought of Eden as a particularly riveting part of God's Story. A necessary introduction, yes, but not exactly spellbinding. Thoughts of Eden conjure up mental images of Adam and Eve strolling leisurely through the garden hand-in-hand—picking flowers, popping grapes, working without sweat. No weeds, insects, or plant diseases to interfere with their gardening projects. No battle of the sexes or angry words spoken in haste and regretted later. Sex and nudity notwithstanding, the story seems a bit dull—at least until the serpent shows up and all hell breaks loose. Judging by what literary experts are saying about conflict, before the fall Adam and Eve are living in a *plotless* story.

Which made me wonder, if God is the master storyteller—the creator of story—and if conflict *makes* the story, is there conflict *before* Genesis 3? Was God's original vision for us and for the world a plotless story? If humanity had never fallen into sin, would we be living in a *plotless* story now? For that matter, will heaven be plotless? Is conflict only and always destructive and the result of fallenness? Or is there a *healthy, necessary, constructive* variety of conflict that creates a gripping plot and is designed to make God's image bearers flourish and grow?

Four words, given in pairs, contain the essence of humanity's mission: "*fruitful*" and "*multiply*" and "*rule*" and "*subdue*."[5] It's hard to believe how easily we breeze past these foundational creation commands on which both God's purposes for us and the good of the planet ride. I confess, I've brushed past them many times myself, never realizing that I've been walking past yet another explosive concept that if I slowed my pace and took a closer look would rock my world. This is no minor offense, for by glossing over what God is saying we fail to take him seriously. We have been charging forward presumptuously without weighing instructions designed to shape our lives and advance his kingdom.

Historically, fruitful and multiply have been understood to mean physical reproduction or populating the earth—something necessary for survival. How strange, then, that reproduction has come to be regarded as a problem by Christians and non-Christians alike. Not every pregnancy is celebrated. Octomom made headlines for bringing fourteen lives into the world, but she was not heralded as an icon of fruitfulness. Rather, she was publicly vilified for recklessly overdoing it. The human race has been so successful at reproducing, many nations are now investing millions in sex education, contraceptives, and support for abortions, all to reduce the number of pregnancies brought to term. On the flip side, not every woman is able or wants to give birth. Apart from extraordinary medical measures that occasionally have women over fifty giving birth, the average woman has a smaller window of fertility when reproduction is possible. If the command to be fruitful and multiply is only about reproduction, then it can apply only to a short season in a woman's life—her window of childbearing years.

Rule and subdue do not usually form part of the Christian picture of a woman. These Genesis words are mainly associated with the high status of God's image bearers as lords over creation and our responsibility to develop and steward earth's resources. Some think it has reference to environmentalism — which resonates with my Oregonian roots. Most often rule and subdue have become fodder in the ongoing debate over gender differences, roles, and equality. The tendency of scholars to retain *masculine* nouns and pronouns in this part of the discussion sometimes leads female and male readers to assume God is only addressing men, when in fact he is addressing *both* of his image bearers. The question arises: Is God calling women to rule and subdue too? And if he is, what is that supposed to look like?

One thing is clear: we are not in Eden anymore. A lot has happened since then. We have more to go on than the first two chapters of Genesis — more history and all of Scripture to help us understand what God had in mind when he issued those first commands. But by far the most important piece of the puzzle and the source of greatest clarity are the earthly life and ministry of Jesus, who walked among us and showed us how to bear God's image in this fallen world.

Whatever we lost in Eden we find again in Jesus. Whatever God meant by "fruitful and multiply" and "rule and subdue," Jesus fulfills. As God's perfect image bearer, Jesus recaptures God's original vision for us by embodying true image-bearer living. And Jesus didn't do this in the pristine, sin-free garden our first parents inhabited, but in the fallen ruins of the world we occupy. Jesus is the missing chapter in Genesis.

We will never grasp the richness of what it means to be fruitful and multiply or to rule and subdue in isolation from him. Jesus — who never married or had physical children of his own and who surprisingly endorses singleness (as did the apostle Paul), not simply as an unfortunate consequence of a fallen world but as a kingdom strategy.[6] Jesus — who is

King of kings and Lord of all, yet whose ruling and subduing take on a shockingly unfamiliar form from what we typically observe in people who occupy positions of power and privilege over others. Jesus — who when asked what is the greatest commandment, didn't answer "be fruitful and multiply ... rule and subdue," but " 'You must love the Lord your God with all your heart, all your soul, all your mind, and all your strength,' " adding, "The second is equally important: 'Love your neighbor as yourself.' No other commandment is greater than these" (Mark 12:30–31). Somehow, all of these elements inform and shape the mission God gave us in the beginning.

MULTIPLYING GOD'S IMAGE

So, yes, to be fruitful and multiply means physical reproduction. The same two words are used for sea creatures and birds (Genesis 1:20–22). Fish multiply fish. Birds multiply birds. But we are not fish or birds. We are God's image bearers. And while physical reproduction may suffice for fish and birds, for image bearers multiplication involves far more than simply populating the earth with more people. God calls us *to multiply image bearers* — a new humanity that embraces the God who made us and whose purpose is for his will to be done on earth as it is in heaven. Multiplying for us moves beyond the purely biological to a much deeper and more challenging spiritual command that calls *every* image bearer to engage. The outcome of this kind of multiplying means that God's glory spreads over the planet as his image bearers reflect his attributes — his goodness, mercy, love and justice, truth and grace, and more — wherever they are.

Fruitfulness is a major biblical theme that points to the results or "fruit" of our faithfulness to God. When coupled with "multiply," fruitfulness does connote *physical reproduc-*

tion.[7] But as theologian Stanley J. Grenz makes clear, "pro-creation may possibly be a functional dimension of the image and consequently in some sense serve as an analogy to God's creative action."[8] If, as Grenz suggests, God's creative activity in calling the world into being is the model for human creativity, then we too are called *to live creative and productive lives.* Andy Crouch echoes this idea when he says of the Genesis 1 narrative, "splashed all over the page is God's purposeful and energetic desire to create. So when the human beings, male and female, are created 'in God's image,' surely the primary implication is that they will reflect the creative character of their Maker."[9] By identifying the greatest commandment as loving God with all we are, Jesus reinforces this message by calling us to vigorous, creative, full-throttled living.

Ruling and subduing are strong expressions that place a weighty responsibility on us to look after all creation on God's behalf and to persevere against the resistance that comes from the Enemy. C. S. Lewis would no doubt say, "God has made us Kings and Queens of Narnia." This is a call to leadership according to the Jesus model, which is not about power, authority, or elbowing our way past others to climb to the top, but the self-giving, costly, kingdom-minded leadership of Jesus.[10]

The psalmist unpacks what ruling under God entails, for a ruler after God's own heart will "rescue the poor when they cry to him … the oppressed, who have no one to defend them. He feels pity for the weak and the needy, and he will rescue them. He will redeem them from oppression and violence, for their lives are precious to him" (Psalm 72:12–14). The net effect of God's command to rule and subdue is a clarion call to leadership—to govern and look after God's creation. It means that what happens in this world is our business. God expects us to pay attention and become activists on his behalf to aid those who need our advocacy and help.

That these four commands show up so early in the Story is slightly alarming, for it suggests that even *before* the fall — *before* the world became a mess — building a kingdom wasn't easy. God was summoning his image bearers into battle on behalf of his creation. Resistance made it necessary for them to be resourceful, strong, and unrelenting in their efforts to obey. These four commands help us understand that conflict was in God's Story before the first act of human history commenced. God gave his two image bearers a global mission that dwarfs our resources — a task that surely had them exchanging wide-eyed worried glances. Contrary to what we may have assumed, fulfilling these four commands won't happen without diligent and courageous effort.

Before sin enters the human experience, God's Story is loaded with conflict — but it is a healthy conflict designed to draw his image bearers out and bless the world. But that isn't all.

THE PLOT THICKENS

Read the Genesis story again. Start from "in the beginning God created" and freeze the action just as Eve and Adam are about to sink their teeth into the forbidden fruit — *before* they sin. Conflict is already there — lots of conflict. Already we can see that God's image bearers are not trusting him. They are doubting and asking the kinds of hard questions that have plagued the human race ever since: Is God good? Can we be sure of him? Does he have our best interests at heart or is he holding out on us? Is he for or against us?

The relationship between them isn't what it is supposed to be either. Despite Adam's jubilant "bone-of-my-bones" poetry, they do not present a united front against the Enemy. They aren't collaborating and standing together. There is no iron sharpening iron here. Clearly the beautiful union God had in mind when he brought male and female together isn't automatic. And for the Enemy to get past security and be inside the garden converts the paradisiacal Eden into a dangerous war zone. The threat level in Eden escalates to a blazing hot red—*before* the fall.

Even in a perfect world, *before* sin enters the picture, conflict is in the story. We are mistaken to think God ushered Adam and Even into a plotless life. Even in their sinless state, earth's first two human inhabitants had room to mature and grow. There was work to be done. They had relationships to build with God and with each other and a kingdom mission that required everything they had to give, not to mention a powerful Enemy lurking in the shadows.

Of course, God created the perfect environment in which his image bearers could thrive and grow. He didn't create a flat earth. God's world has mountains that awaken in us the need to climb, to test our limits and find out firsthand what it's like to stand atop a snowy peak. He created a world that is packed with endless treasure, raw material, and unexplored frontiers designed to stir up in us the artist, the scientist, the explorer-adventurer, the athlete, the mathematician, the botanist, the entrepreneur, and much more. He didn't give the world's first residents a furnished apartment within driving distance of a shopping mall. God placed them—without a stitch of clothing or a roof over their heads—in a garden and challenged them to make a life for themselves. To underscore his intentions, he spread before them the whole earth and commanded them to look after it on his behalf.

The world seemingly was waiting for God's image bearers to put their creative powers to work—to create culture and civilization, the arts, sciences, and technology. The world was made for our flourishing and for the earth to flourish under our care. Even the expansive skies overhead beckoned. Did those first two image bearers imagine flying—or journeying to the moon? The brand of conflict that existed prior to the fall doesn't hinder the image bearer's mission in the world; it actually fuels and accelerates its accomplishment.

Earth was a cosmic ball of raw material. And God's image bearers are raw material too. God has put within reach everything we need (including himself) to thrive and grow and develop the potential for which he created us. In each of us he has implanted the seeds of creativity and curiosity, and the hunger to learn that drive us forward. I love the thought that we never know when we celebrate the birth of a child whether we are welcoming the next Picasso, the future world leader who will finally negotiate peace in the Middle East, or the brilliant scientist whose efforts will produce the cure to cancer. It remains to be seen what each small bundle of life will do with the gifts and opportunities God bestows. It remains to be seen what they will do to cultivate their likeness to God as his image bearers. Conflict—healthy, constructive, kingdom strategic conflict—will draw them out.

THE GIRL EFFECT

The Care International video doesn't end with "The world is a mess." It goes on to identify an "unexpected solution" to poverty, AIDS, hunger, and war. The solution? A girl—who with education and a microloan can buy a cow, start a business, and help her family. As her small business grows, the benefits ripple beyond her family to her community, improving her neighbor's lives with jobs, clean water, reduced infant mortality, and education—which in turn combine to reduce poverty and boost the local economy.

Greg Mortenson, humanitarian founder of the Central

Asia Institute that builds schools for children in Pakistan and Afghanistan, reports the same thing. "Once you educate the boys, they tend to leave the villages and go search for work in the cities. But the girls stay home, become leaders in the community, and pass on what they've learned. If you really want to change a culture, to empower women, improve basic hygiene and health care, and fight high rates of infant mortality, the answer is to educate girls."[11] Mortenson is even convinced that educating girls is a more effective way of combating terrorism than warfare. Kristof's and WuDunn's research confirms this perspective:

> Some security experts noted that the countries that nurture terrorists are disproportionally those where women are marginalized. The reason there are so many Muslim terrorists, they argued, has little to do with the Koran but a great deal to do with the lack of robust female participation in the economy and society of many Islamic countries. As the Pentagon gained a deeper understanding of counterterrorism, and as it found that dropping bombs often didn't do much to help, it became increasingly interested in grassroots projects such as girls' education. Empowering girls, some in the military argued, would disempower terrorists.[12]

None of this should surprise us. The notion that "Women hold up half the sky" can be traced back a whole lot earlier than the twentieth century and Mao Zedong. It can be found on the opening pages of the Bible, where God calls *both* men and women to hold up the sky together by becoming compassionate, proactive leaders who look after things in this world for him. God created both his sons and his daughters to rule with justice and mercy and to fight the battles necessary to subdue and push back the forces of evil that threaten us on all sides.

I believe the church of Jesus Christ should be *first in line* to champion the empowerment of women and girls throughout the world to become contributing members in their societies. In fact, the community of God's people should be the epicenter of human flourishing—where men and women are encouraged and supported in their efforts to develop and use the gifts God has given them wherever he stations them in his world. The church of Jesus Christ should be such a dazzling showpiece of female and male flourishing that the world will take notice.

God never envisioned a world where his image bearers would do life in low gear or be encouraged to hold back, especially when suffering is rampant, people are lost, and there is so much kingdom work to do. He wants his daughters to thrive, mature, gain wisdom, hone their gifts, and contribute to his vast purposes in our world. We should be the first to celebrate the news that the doors of education and opportunity are opening to young girls who are emerging as leaders and who are blessing their communities and improving national economies. Isn't this at least part of what it means for God's will to be done on earth?

I have sat in women's conferences where Christian women are soothed with messages telling them they matter, that God thinks they're beautiful, and that they need to carve out time alone with God. I'm all for encouragement and am passionate about challenging women to go deeper in the study of God's Word. But that message *must* be accompanied by the call to step out, to engage this world, and to make it better for all.

God created his daughters to be kingdom builders—to pay attention to what is happening around us, to take action and contribute. Commands to multiply image bearers, to live productive lives, to rule the whole earth, and to subdue the Enemy's efforts are aimed at women too. Let us not miss

God's original vision, namely, that *he is raising up his daughters to be leaders.* That idea is explicit in his command to rule and subdue—a command that doesn't leave out a single square inch of this earth. In the beginning, God envisioned a world of leaders and hardwired leadership into his image bearers' DNA—the DNA of his daughters as well as his sons.

The Bible doesn't blink (even though some Christians may) when Deborah, Esther, Mary of Nazareth, Priscilla, Phoebe, and Junia emerge as strong, courageous leaders. The world is a better place, and God's kingdom surges forward because of strong godly leaders like these women. What impresses me is how many women exercise courageous kingdom leadership and carry God's purposes forward *beyond the spotlight* where their undeniable leadership can easily escape our notice. Naomi, Ruth, Hannah, Tamar, Rahab, and Mary Magdalene are just a few of many striking examples.

The definition of leadership according to Jesus is radical and potent. His brand of leadership doesn't mean having a following or being popular. Often it means standing alone, feeling isolated and fearful, but doing what is right in God's sight anyway, regardless of what others think. Kingdom leadership doesn't mean being first, but being last. It's not about being the boss, but showing indiscriminate grace to others—even those who wrong us, even when it goes against the natural grain of our hearts. This is how God's kingdom advances.

I can't speak for anyone else, but I find God's vision exhilarating and sobering—and not the way we typically see ourselves. Jesus' parable of the talents sends a double message: that what we do with our lives matters to him and that Jesus takes a dim view when anyone buries their talents and opportunities in the ground instead of using them.

There's no age requirement for kingdom building and no expiration date when we retire. No square inch of this planet is beyond the scope of our kingdom responsibilities. We may retire from our jobs. The nest may empty. We may lose our health. But God's image bearers remain on active duty. I've known young girls who were steadfastly kingdom minded and elderly women in nursing homes who were diligently going about God's business when the clock ran out. God never retires his image bearers.

Conflict is in God's Story and has been from the beginning. And conflict is in our stories. There's no escaping it. But what is surprising is to see just how God turns the conflict that we think is pulling us to pieces to serve his constructive purposes for his image bearers—to draw us out and shape us into leaders. God uses conflict to shape a leader's soul, as we are about to see.

DISCUSSION QUESTIONS

1. Why is conflict necessary to make a great story, and why is there no plot without it?

2. What kinds of healthy, necessary, constructive conflict existed before Adam and Eve sinned, and how was conflict designed to draw them out?

3. How does God's command to "be fruitful and multiply" mean more than sexual reproduction?

4. What does it mean for you to "rule and subdue," and what are some ways you are already doing that?

5. Describe how God has used conflict in your life to help you grow and change.

CHAPTER 4

THE SHAPING
OF A LEADER'S SOUL

She was only four years old and they were going to burn her!

A child in India at the tender age of four was already legally married, although she still lived with her parents and had no clue what it all meant. When her much older "husband" died suddenly, this little four-year-old became a widow. Instead of skipping off to preschool, like little girls we know, this tiny child widow was destined for *sati*—to be burned to ashes on her husband's funeral pyre. *Sati*, a Hindu ritual outlawed decades ago (although cases have been documented since), is one of the world's most appalling value statements of a woman. Sometimes women buy into *sati*. Widows have been known voluntarily to immolate themselves as an act of ultimate marital fidelity, sometimes in hopes of securing salvation for their dead husbands.[1] In the case of this little girl, however, *sati* wasn't a choice or a so-called "noble" act. It was an execution.

For some widows, staying alive is worse than *sati*. In India still today "the loss of a husband can be an upheaval beyond belief ... a one-way ticket to isolation, poverty, and despair."[2] In cultures where a woman's identity depends on her attachment to a male, "widowhood has a much larger dimension than losing a husband."[3] Without a husband, she has no value and can be thrown out as an unnecessary encumbrance, even by her own children. Streets in some cities are filled with homeless widows. Younger outcast widows are often subjected to sexual abuse and trafficking. Chances are slim to none for uneducated widows to improve their circumstances or to pursue any legal rights that the government grants them.

REAL, BUT UNLIKELY WOMEN LEADERS

In speaking of women as leaders, doesn't it make more sense to choose a woman from the Bible's impressive lineup of recognized female leaders — someone like Miriam, Deborah, Esther, Huldah, Mary, Priscilla, Phoebe, or Junia (and that's just the short list)? Not necessarily. Having delved deeply into the lives of Ruth and Naomi in *The Gospel of Ruth*,[4] I can't think of two better candidates for this discussion *precisely* because they were so unlikely. Had I chosen a woman known for her leadership achievements, I would be reinforcing conventional ideas of leadership, as those who rise to the top and have titles, a following, and public recognition to go with their achievements. I am certain this would cause a good number of female readers to place themselves on the edges of this discussion and assume I'm talking about someone else.

Naomi and Ruth represent the lowest common denominator when it comes to women, and to see how they evolved as leaders will challenge our assumptions about women as leaders and invite us all into the conversation. Whatever we conclude about them as leaders applies to all of us. The very nature of their circumstances injects an intriguing degree of uncertainty as to where this discussion is going.

As a starting point, there's no denying the fact that women do emerge as strong leaders in the Bible, complete with titles, recognition, and high praise. At the very least, this raises the possibility that to resist thinking of ourselves as leaders is to stiff-arm something important that God is calling us to do. But there is this other undeniable fact—that being God's image bearer, whether you are male or female, comes with significant leadership responsibilities, as we saw in the previous chapter. God created and is counting on his image bearers to be active on his behalf.

Here is the point. The Bible doesn't merely leave the door ajar for *some* women to become leaders; it actually makes a rather emphatic case that God *expects* his daughters to be leaders. A lot is riding on our willingness to see this. It is not overstating things to say that there are dire global repercussions if half the church reluctantly backs away from something this important or imagines that this only concerns a select group of women and the male half of the church. This is not to advocate anarchy, insurrection, or disregard for the authority structures we all live within, nor does it create a scenario where we are all pulling in different directions. Rather, it is to redefine leadership in kingdom/gospel terms.

The Bible gives us leadership examples that won't let any of us off the hook; this is where Naomi and Ruth come in. No one would imagine that God was raising up the two beleaguered souls who reentered Bethlehem to become kingdom leaders. They take us to a place where no headhunter would think of going in search of leaders, to the forgotten backroom where a widow retires from meaningful activity and others think nothing of throwing her out with the trash. Ironically, though they are counted out by everyone else (including themselves), they are counted *in* by God.

LEADERSHIP ON THE LINE

I thought of Boaz when I read about a study that Hunter College psychology professor Virginia Valian conducted on leadership. She presented a group of students with a series of slides picturing five people sitting at a table—one at the head and two on either side. She asked the students to identify the leader. When the people at the table were all men or all women, students always pointed to the person at the head of the table. But if the people were both male and female and a woman sat at the head of the table, half the time students chose a man who sat on the side.[5] So even in the secular world, there's at least a subterranean assumption that if men are present, they will naturally take the lead.

That assumption governs how we tend to look at the book of Ruth. After meeting the trio of main characters in the Ruth story—Naomi, Ruth, and Boaz—it doesn't matter how they're seated around the table; most readers point to Boaz as the obvious leader among the three. He is an imposing figure who exudes leadership and who, for all the right reasons, *deserves* to be admired. Described as a man of valor (*ḥayil*),[6] he may well have been a decorated military hero. He's an Israelite blue-blood and has the pedigree to prove it. The most luminous person in his family tree is his grandfather Nahshon, Judah's tribal leader, the third male in command after Moses and Aaron. Like a Kennedy or a Windsor, Boaz has leadership in his blood. He was born to lead, and from the look of things, he is upholding the family legacy.

By contrast, one quick glance at Naomi would lead anyone to conclude that "leadership" and "Naomi" don't belong in the same sentence. She enters the story on the arm of her husband, Elimelech, a member of Israel's leading tribe of Judah, and they are accompanied by their two sons. Her boys are Naomi's résumé, representing her accomplishments as a woman and her contributions to the world. According to patriarchal standards, she has succeeded as a woman for she has borne her husband two sons. They are the crown of her womanhood—a double guarantee that the family will survive for another generation. That's what her culture expects of a woman. Naomi literally has delivered. A comfortable retirement and the laughter of grandchildren are in her future. But leadership?

Then conflict invades Naomi's story with a ruthlessness that is hard to believe, wiping out everything that gives meaning to her life. When the dust clears, nothing is left of her. She doesn't face *sati*, but her résumé is torched. Naomi's contemporaries squint and struggle to recognize the shattered remnants of the woman they once knew. With the expiration of her childbearing years, Naomi has nothing left to contribute. Anyone in search of leaders would pass over Naomi without a second thought.

Ruth's qualifications are just as bad, if not a little worse. Her résumé informs us she is Gentile, pagan, and female. With credentials like that, she has no business being in a very Jewish, very male story like the one unfolding in the Old Testament—certainly not as a leader. She enters the story anyway through a side door by marrying one of Naomi's sons. Some speculate that Ruth was a Moabite princess, but that seems doubtful, for no high-ranking Moabite father in his right mind would stoop to marry his daughter to a foreign famine refugee. He'd be squandering an opportunity to forge an advantageous alliance with another prominent family. A more realistic guess is that Ruth was a leftover daughter—a financial burden her family was eager to off-load. We'd like to think she was a dazzling, dark-eyed beauty, but the only physical description we have is of a woman strong enough to carry a load of sixty to a hundred pounds.[7] As an immigrant inside Israelite borders, the safest and smartest thing for her to do in Bethlehem is to maintain a low profile. To imagine herself a leader could be asking for trouble.

Compared to Naomi and Ruth (who only bring deficiencies to the table), Boaz is a powerhouse and holds all the cards. He has wealth, power, and stature, and he is male. Yet, contrary to first impressions, leadership arises from unexpected sources, and Boaz will be taking cues from others. Remarkably, he will become a better and a different kind of leader when conflict and two women leaders invade his life.

Conflict brings this trio together in nitro-meets-glycerin combinations that create the explosive and hair-raising headlines we hear *every* day. Male meets female, haves meet have-nots, privilege meets destitution, power meets powerlessness, Israeli meets Arab, and native son meets immigrant. Yet from this explosive mixture, something wholly unexpected and sacred bursts forth: kingdom leadership at its best.

CAUGHT IN THE CONFLICT

So how does the story unfold? Tragedy explodes on the scene in the first five verses of the book of Ruth, sweeping all three characters into conflict. The devastation is so extensive, so complete, that the opening sentences sound more like the ending than the beginning of the story. Without a word of explanation or the slightest hint of God's interference, Naomi's whole world collapses under the cumulative weight of a series of heart-wrenching tragedies. By far, the most devastating losses are the deaths of her husband and *both* of her sons, for with their deaths, so dies the family, leaving Naomi an empty shell of the woman she used to be. Proponents of *sati* would no doubt remark that there is not enough left of her to make much of a fire.

Marriage to Mahlon is the link that pulls Ruth into the crisis, for by the time those first five verses have finished, Ruth is empty too. The future holds only misery for her. Had her husband lived, most likely Ruth would be making room for wife number two and *his* second chance at progeny. Without him, she faces a life of hardship and an endless struggle to survive. Either way, her suffering is compounded by the public shame of failing to produce a son for her husband after ten years of trying. I think of Ruth when I read stories of child widows in today's world. A life sentence of ostracism, poverty, and worthlessness is an appalling fate for anyone. It's a stiffer punishment when handed down to the young. The best scholarly estimates are that Ruth was probably widowed somewhere in her early twenties.

But much to the surprise of readers—especially the original readers of this story—what sounds like the end of the story is actually the beginning. In contrast to what typically happens to widows in many corners of the world, these two widows command center stage and do so without the necessary male connections to justify why they are there. The biblical camera zooms in and this conflict-riddled story continues. "God is in the business of using the unlikely to perform the holy."[8] There's no predicting whom he will chose to act on his behalf in powerful ways, and we are mistaken to rule anybody out.

CONFLICT WITH GOD

The conflict that impacts Naomi's life centers on her brokenness. "In a way, every grief is two-dimensional—the loss itself along with the nagging thought that it could have been prevented if only God had acted."[9] Naomi's losses are irre-placeable. Once full of life and of family, accomplishments, and honor, tragedy has hollowed her out. Here the decibel of grief and pain cannot be measured, God seems more enemy than friend, and anger rises in Naomi with volcanic force. Brokenness and loss draw her into a ferocious and utterly important conflict with God that puts her squarely into the company of Job. Ironically, despite angry outbursts and the cloud of despair that hangs overhead, conflict's kingdom powers have already gained the upper hand. Instead of driv-ing a wedge between Naomi and God, as we might expect, conflict drives her to him.

Naomi's belief that God has turned against her reinforces the messages coming to her from the culture and from her own despairing soul. She doesn't matter. She is worthless. She has nothing to contribute. Her life is over. But in the midst of this deafening chorus of voices, one solitary voice dares to contradict the others — that voice belongs to Ruth. When Naomi is feeling most forsaken on the road to Bethlehem, she is held in Ruth's stubborn embrace as she hears her daughter-in-law speak fierce words of ḥesed. [10] "Don't ask me to leave you and turn back. Wherever you go, I will go; wherever you live, I will live. Your people will be my people, and your God will be my God. Wherever you die, I will die, and there I will be buried. May the LORD punish me severely if I allow anything but death to separate us!" (Ruth 1:16–17). Ruth is God's image bearer. She speaks and acts for him.

The message finally gets through to Naomi at the end of a long, anxious day of waiting for Ruth to return from her first day of gleaning. Ruth arrives home that evening, not bat-tered, bruised, and sobbing, but bearing twenty-nine pounds of winnowed barley — an impossibly large harvest for one day of gleaning.[11] Naomi's reaction confirms C. S. Lewis's assertion that "God whispers to us in our pleasures ... but shouts in our pains."[12] Something she never would have noticed in more prosperous times is shouting at her from an ordinary pile of barley. God has not forsaken her. Indeed his *hesed* for Naomi has never been stronger. It is a powerful turning point for Naomi.

CONFLICT WITH SELF

Unlike Naomi, Ruth doesn't provide many clues that give us a window on her soul. Her story overlaps with Naomi's in many ways, for she shares the losses, the emptiness of childless widowhood, and a future of grinding poverty. But unlike Naomi, Ruth doesn't reveal her feelings in a stormy outburst, but in subtle hints that surface in her interactions with Boaz.

In their first encounter, when Ruth boldly requests permission to glean in a more fruitful part of the field that is off-limits to gleaners, Boaz's unexpected kindness elicits this response from her: "You have *comforted* me by speaking so kindly to me, even though I am not one of your workers" (Ruth 2:13; emphasis added).[13] Later, at the threshing floor, where she really crosses the line by confronting Boaz with legal responsibilities to Naomi, Boaz tells her, "Don't be afraid" (3:11).

More was taking place back on the road from Moab than an intense debate over Ruth's travel itinerary. At that moment, Ruth was changing sides in the great cosmic battle between the kingdom of God and the kingdom of this fallen world. By embracing Naomi and Naomi's God, Ruth exchanges one compass for another. Now Yahweh is her north star, and the compass she relies on from here on is pointing her to him. Although she has come under Yahweh's wing, he does not lead her to a life of complacency or resignation. The road ahead will push her out of her comfort zone and into the path of a powerful, larger-than-life man whose actions cannot be predicted and who holds the power to grant or refuse her unconventional requests. Fear stands in her way. Lest we minimize Ruth's reason for fear—even in Bethlehem among God's people—the biblical record sets us straight.

Half the Sky documents accounts of women who go to the police to report they've been raped, and instead of coming to their defense, the police rape them again.[14] It is frightening when the person to whom a woman appeals for help becomes the enemy. Writers of Scripture record appalling crimes against women that rival the shocking stories journalists are reporting today.

It is worth reminding ourselves that brutality and injustice against women ignite the outrage of Yahweh and his prophets. The prophet Amos is beside himself in expressing God's fury over the trafficking of human beings. Isaiah lashes out against corruption among the powerful and the injustices they inflict on the powerless. "Woe to those who ... deprive the poor of their rights and withhold justice from the oppressed of my people, making widows their prey and robbing the fatherless" (Isaiah 10:1–2 NIV). And again, "Your rulers are rebels, companions of thieves; they all love bribes and chase after gifts. They do not defend the cause of the fatherless; the widow's case does not come before them" (1:23 NIV).

Both Boaz and Naomi make statements that give us a realistic picture of life in Bethlehem and of the dangers Ruth risked when she ventured out as a lone female gleaner. Without stern intervention, even Boaz's field wasn't the safest place to be. When Boaz granted her special gleaning privileges that would bring her into close proximity with his male harvesters, he raised a necessary shield of protection around her when he said, "I have told the men not to touch you" (Ruth

2:9). On hearing this, Naomi urged Ruth to continue working in his fields, "because in someone else's field you might be harmed" (Ruth 2:22). *Half the Sky*'s disturbing stories are not far from the mark.

For Ruth, following God means she must take the initiative, assume the lead, and violate a lifetime of cultural conditioning and upbringing, long-established behavioral patterns, and the expectations she has internalized for how a proper female should behave. If she was anything like the rest of us, to call this stressful is an understatement. Given the risks of venturing out into the fields of Bethlehem and later to the threshing floor, it would be forgivable if Ruth chose to spend the rest of her life in seclusion. But she has already stepped beyond the safety zone by pledging herself to Naomi and to Yahweh.

CONFLICT OF INTEREST

Gary Haugen, President and CEO of International Justice Mission, defines injustice as the *abuse of power*—a worldwide plague where the strong prey on the weak. One of the common examples he cites has chilling implications for Naomi and Ruth. "Wealthy landowners rob widows of their land, livelihood and dignity."[15] Abuse of power is a double-edged sword, where selfish *actions* as well as selfish *inaction* cause God's image bearers grossly to misrepresent him.

Space here doesn't permit a full discussion of the complexities of Boaz's situation, so a brief synopsis must suffice. In sum, Boaz is legally beyond the reach of Mosaic law. His land is open to gleaners, so he is in full compliance with the letter of the gleaning law. He is *not* the nearest kinsman, so is exempt from kinsman-redeemer obligations.[16] He is *not* Elimelech's brother, so the levirate law[17] does not apply to him either. But the levirate law is irrelevant anyway because Naomi (the widow in question) is postmenopausal.

Boaz, along with other men in Elimelech's tribe, are in for some measure of criticism for not doing voluntarily what they could to assist Naomi and Ruth, which in God's eyes represents a passive abuse of power. But the fact remains: Boaz answers to no one for how he responds to Ruth and can do what he wills with impunity. Ruth is brash enough to place all three above-mentioned laws before Boaz and call him to fulfill their spirit—to feed the poor and to rescue the family and the property of Elimelech. Her proposal goes beyond what the law requires, and the law itself calls for the major outlay of Boaz's resources, including himself. She asks of Boaz what he is under no legal obligation to do. But Boaz's compass is trained on Yahweh too, and so instead of dismissing this foreign newcomer's words out of hand, Boaz experiences a healthy conflict of interest. What will he do with his advantages? How will he exercise his power?

LEADERS FORGED BY CONFLICT

Three separate tracks converge at the threshing floor scene in an extraordinary confluence of sacrificial love, and it is conflict that draws them together. Conflict draws kingdom leadership out of all three. Their focus is outward. They are paying attention to what is happening around them and looking out for others. They accept responsibility to do whatever they can to remedy the situation—even if it costs them everything. Three lives are on the line. Kingdom issues are at stake that go well beyond what these three individuals will ever see. They are focused on the pressing issues of the present.

But what this trio does to make a difference now will ripple far beyond their localized circumstances and the people in their purview. The world and all eternity will feel the impact. "As Yahweh's 'called-out ones,' his people become God's gift to the world … agents of God's work and continued concern to his world … a community focused on 'the other' rather than on 'self.' "[18]

Conflict moves Naomi to radical advocacy for Ruth. Ruth's gift of barley is Naomi's epiphany. Confident in God's *hesed* in deeper ways than she ever imagined God's love, she is standing on solid rock. What she has seen of God in the blackness of her brokenness frees her from self-absorbed grief to turn her attention to Ruth. Naomi comes out of herself and takes the lead. Time is running out. What will become of Ruth when Naomi is gone? In an act of extraordinary sacrifice—a true act of *hesed*—Naomi initiates a plan to secure Ruth's future. Her intention is for Ruth to come under the protective umbrella of a husband, even if it means Naomi will be left alone. Boaz's kindness to Ruth as gleaner gives Naomi hope that he will have compassion and take Ruth as his wife.

Naomi is not playing matchmaker. A man of honor like Boaz would never abuse his powers or dishonor his family by looking for romance among destitute gleaners. And it would be the height of cruelty and selfishness for Naomi to send her barren daughter-in-law on a mission to bear a child. Romantic diehards may resist, but this was a polygamous culture. Bachelors don't exist in patriarchal cultures, or if they do, they bring shame upon their family for refusing to produce sons. A man of Boaz's age (Naomi's generation)[19] and sterling reputation was almost certainly already married with sons. The only prayer for a young woman in Ruth's circumstances is to become an extra pair of hands to help in the household, if Boaz will show her mercy. In the absence of a male to negotiate a marriage, Naomi sends Ruth to the threshing floor at night with detailed instructions designed to ensure her safety and communicate to Boaz that she is proposing marriage.

Conflict ignites radical courage in Ruth. Simply following Naomi's instructions to go to the sleeping Boaz, uncover his feet, lie down, and wait for him to tell her what to do demands enormous courage. But Ruth has not come to the threshing floor for herself. She has come here for Naomi. Ruth will not forget the vow she made to stick with Naomi through thick and thin. She isn't about to start living for herself now. Instead of seeking security for herself, Ruth tosses out Naomi's game plan for an agenda of her own.

Ruth's purpose is not to find a husband for herself but to rescue Naomi's family from extinction. Instead of waiting for Boaz's instruction, Ruth instructs Boaz. She presents a gutsy marriage proposal to Boaz with all sorts of outrageous strings attached, both for her and for him. Her proposal is tantamount to laying down her own life as a surrogate widow for Naomi (a breathtaking act of faith, given her infertility) and recruiting Boaz to join her in rescuing the family of Elimelech. Here Ruth becomes the ultimate risk-taker, and Boaz, faced with a staggering demand on his resources, will prove to be her match.

Instead of the simple decision of whether to add another wife to support, Boaz is confronted with the obligation—well beyond the scope of the law—to drain significant funds from his estate to rehabilitate Elimelech's. Ruth's proposal is highly irregular, which is the first hurdle Boaz must cross. But in doing that, Boaz will also cross over from the letter of the law to its spirit and from an earthbound obedience to God to true kingdom living.

The second hurdle involves enormous risk, for Ruth is proposing a high-stakes gamble for Boaz that is potentially lucrative or financially disastrous, depending on whether Ruth gives birth to a son. If Boaz agrees and she remains barren, his sons stand to inherit a lot more. But if she has a son, all of Boaz's investments will go to Elimelech's new heir. Any potential kinsman redeemer understands precisely what risks are involved. The nearer kinsman helps us understand the issues facing Boaz when he refuses the offer, saying, "I can't redeem it … because this might endanger my own estate. You redeem the land; I cannot do it" (Ruth 4:6).

Conflict summons Boaz to radical obedience. "Spread the corner of your garment over me, since you are a kinsman-redeemer" (Ruth 3:9). Startled awake in the dead of night by the presence of a woman lying at his feet, this man of impeccable integrity discovers once again from Ruth that there is far more to God's law than complying with the letter. Pharisaical tendencies in all of us make the walk of faith doable. We can be moral, go to church, read our Bibles, and give our 10 percent. Jesus and Ruth knock down the walls of that kind of thinking. Real kingdom living is costly. It will stretch, bend, and break us. Following Jesus isn't the path to a tame or easy life. It is about taking up a cross—which means laying down our lives as Jesus did for the sake of others.

Boaz has an escape hatch—actually more than one—that he will deliberately refuse to use. The image bearer who reflects God's *hesed* will not take the easy way out. The conflict of interest is intense but short-lived for Boaz. He gets it that she is rescuing the family and, in an act that mirrors her *hesed*, he throws his full weight behind her rescue effort. And if for only a brief moment, the world witnesses an Oscar-winning moment as three image bearers display kingdom leadership and join forces to display God's *hesed* to the world. Kingdoms are in collision—the kingdom of the world versus the kingdom of heaven—and God's kingdom has won out.

LEADERSHIP RE-ENVISIONED

In today's world, where growing numbers of women and men take it for granted that women can and should be leaders, women who already hold leadership positions or who aspire to be leaders might assume this discussion is mainly about them, when in fact, this is a much wider conversation. The Bible's view of leadership is much more radical than opening doors for a few, even though those doors need to open too. But despite changing attitudes in today's world, significant numbers of evangelical Christians remain uncomfortable applying the word "leader" to a woman. They may reluctantly allow for rare "exceptions" here and there. (One can't help calling someone like Amy Carmichael a leader.) But in the main, according to this line of thinking as a general rule leadership is male; following is female.

It is argued that this is the way things are meant to be—the way things have been since the beginning. This conviction runs deep and impacts the message that the church is embracing and exporting for women. It causes women whose kingdom efforts are indispensible in many places to pull back and question their calling as leaders. But let us not forget that in the beginning, God created his daughters to be image bearers, and that necessarily entails a call to leadership. Failure to see this creates problems that are often overlooked—the predicament and even the peril this creates for so many women, not to mention how this hampers the mission of the church.

Our strengths and gifts are not worth much if we allow them to lie dormant. To be honest, it's actually dangerous to think God created us to lean on others. If we do not hone our gifts and live on the ready instead of in a default mode of looking to others, in a crisis or under pressure we are at a loss to use our voices, make decisions, stand our ground, or take the initiative that our circumstances demand. This isn't theory, for even as I write these words I know several women who at this very moment are overwhelmed because the person they have always depended on is gone or unable to take care of things.

But even if life coasts along as smoothly as we expected, the mind-set that leadership is someone else's responsibility means our guard is down and we may not even notice the kingdom battles God is calling us to fight. It is difficult to reconcile any of this with our calling to be God's image bearers. In prosperity, we may get away with letting others do the leading and living with the expectation that others will take care of us. In regions where war, poverty, or atrocities reign, women don't have that luxury. But as image bearers, our job in this world is to be taking care of others. Women who have far less that we do and are up against far more often put us to shame with the all-out effort they are expending for their families and communities. I frankly find it intriguing that conflict draws out of them the leadership and courage that God implanted in his daughters from day one. These women may never have a single follower, and their stories will most likely go untold, but they are rising up as leaders, and their efforts are making a positive difference for many.

FAST FORWARD

You will be relieved to learn, as I was, that the little four-year-old girl escaped *sati*. In the dead of night, her older brother gently awakened her and smuggled her out of town and into the care of Christian missionaries. It can be said that this was more than a rescue, for although the world had counted her out, God was moving behind the scenes to count a little four-year-old girl in. I first heard her hair-raising story from her granddaughter—a vibrant, deeply committed Christian. God chose one small condemned child to raise up multiple generations of believers.

Coming to the end of a chapter like this, there is a gravitational pull—an expectation in Christian circles—to tie things up with a bow, having all the messy pieces put back together again and tacking a suitably upbeat conclusion to the end. I am resisting that urge. Gaining a little perspective on a vast subject like conflict isn't about finding the bright side to suffering or the silver lining behind every cloud. Storybook endings trivialize the ongoing brutal realities for millions of women and little girls—and I cannot trivialize their suffering.

The losses and wounds we suffer in life are deep. They leave lasting scars that are often glossed over by that kind of talk. I have lived a pretty sheltered life compared to the kinds of things other people suffer, and even I wince when someone tries to help me look on the bright side of some of my losses. But for sure, there is no "silver lining" to genocide, abuse, or the trafficking of human lives. There isn't a "bright side" when a four-year-old is abruptly and forever separated from her mother. Talk of salvaging the "good" in some sort of balancing act with evil almost seems sacrilegious and is both hurtful to those who suffer and misguided with respect to the conflict in our stories.

But how can we be honest about the state of things without succumbing to pessimism? How do we look reality in the face without despair? Here's where this is taking me. Whether we live in the beautiful world of Eden, the consummated kingdom of heaven, or this terribly fallen world we're living in now, conflict will *always* be in the Story. God means for his image bearers to reach and grow, to aspire and explore, to find out who he created us to be. Conflict gets us there—even now.

In all of these contexts, conflict reinforces our need for God, drives us to him, forces us to look at him more closely, and deepens our trust. In every chapter of God's Story—the beginning, the fallen middle, and the glorious finale that inaugurates a new beginning—conflict is the plot-maker that pushes us out of the box, out of our comfort zone, out of complacency or resignation or defeat, out of contentment with ourselves and with things as they are—to engage and to live vigorously and deliberately for God's purposes. Conflict brings out the leader in us, transforms our lives from the mundane to the cosmic, and by God's grace forges us into more compassionate, selfless leaders. Conflict in our stories isn't *in* the way; it *is* the way—to becoming better leaders, better image bearers, to creating a better story—to the fulfillment of the Story.

I love what Henry Nouwen says with respect to soul-shaping conflict. In *The Wounded Healer*, he writes, "The great illusion of leadership is to think that [a person] can be led out of the desert by someone who has never been there."[20] Without conflict in our own stories—without being broken ourselves—we are only talking theory to others when we try to lend a hand. Conflict prevents us from becoming a delivery system—bringing words and ideas to others we haven't tested ourselves—instead of joining them on the journey as fellow travelers who struggle too.

If there's still a lingering doubt in your mind that God created his daughters to be strong and to step out with courage for vital kingdom purposes, please keep reading. I think the next chapter may help change your mind.

DISCUSSION QUESTIONS

1. Do you see yourself as a leader? Why or why not?

2. Why does being God's image bearer mean you are a leader? How does Jesus' example redefine what it means to be a leader?

3. How did conflict change Naomi into a leader? Can you relate? Why or why not?

4. How does conflict push Ruth into leadership, and how does she lead Boaz to become a better leader too?

5. Why is it important for you to embrace God's calling on you to be a leader, and what difference could your leadership make for others?

CHAPTER 5

THE *EZER* UNBOUND

She was her father's pride and joy.

A Chinese history professor told his students, "Whatever you say about China is right and wrong at the same time." This is a global paradox. So, for example, wherever we find misogyny, we also will find the basic human reality of a father's love for daughters. What may surprise some readers is that within cultures where the birth of a son triggers wild celebration and the birth of a daughter is greeted with a disappointed hush, there are and have always been fathers who are exceptions to the rule and make no secret of the fact that their daughters are their pride and joy. Three men come to mind: two Muslims and a Jew.

Ali was a Muslim who had come to Oxford from India to study mathematics. Ali and his family lived in the flat two floors down from us in Oxford, and we formed an unexpected friendship that greatly enriched our English adventure. Ali was not a nominal Muslim. He was deeply devout. He even attempted to convert us. His firstborn was a girl—a very bright-eyed and energetic child. Anyone could see how Ali's eyes sparkled with delight whenever his little daughter was near him. Zainab was her father's pride and joy.

Greg Mortenson, in his bestselling book *Three Cups of*

Tea, tells the story of another Muslim, Mohammed Aslam Khan—a story that shatters stereotypes of Muslim men. "I have been blessed nine times," Aslam said. "With five boys and four girls. But my daughter Shakeela is the most clever among them."[1] In a culture where education for girls is opposed, sometimes to the point of extremists dousing and disfiguring girls with acid as they make their way to school, this Pakistani father was unrelenting in his determination to secure an education for his clever daughter. He tracked down Mortenson to see if he might help. Because of her father's perseverance, Shakeela became the first girl in Pakistan's Hushe Valley to enjoy the privilege of a higher education, which paved the way for other girls to go to school. She hopes one day to become a doctor.[2] Shakeela was her father's pride and joy.

Jairus, a contemporary of Jesus whose story appears in the Gospels, had only one child—a daughter. When she was twelve (the year when Jewish families celebrate a boy's coming of age), his little girl lay dying. Although Jairus belonged to a society where rabbis routinely blessed God that they were not born female and it was considered a complete disaster for a man to be without a son, he (like Jesus) was completely out of step with his culture. Instead of bemoaning the fact that his twelve-year-old child wasn't a boy, he was utterly beside himself at the thought of losing her. With the same fierce tenacity as Aslam, Jairus tracked down Jesus to come and heal his precious daughter. She was her father's pride and joy.

Events surrounding the creation of the first woman lead me to believe God harbors those same strong sentiments for his daughters. He greets his first daughter's entry into his Story with not a little fanfare and, in naming her, chooses a name that binds her and all his daughters to himself in a special way. God calls the first woman *ezer*[3]—a name that is used most frequently in the Old Testament for God himself. In a profound sense, God named his firstborn daughter after himself. God is Israel's *ezer*. For God's female image bearers, *ezer* defines a way in which women are uniquely called to reflect God. "Like Father, like daughter," as the saying goes. Our Father is an *ezer*, and we are *ezers* too.

LOSING OXYGEN

On a trip from Orlando to Dallas, Frank and I encountered a string of lengthy delays that threw us completely off schedule. By the time our plane landed at DFW airport, our hosts had been patiently waiting for hours. We bolted off the plane and dashed through the airport and into the revolving glass doors that lead to the baggage claim area, where friends were waiting. I don't know what went wrong, but at that precise moment the revolving doors stopped, and the two of us smacked up against the glass like a couple of bugs on a windshield. Through the glass doors, we could see and hear our hosts laughing.

Reading Genesis 2 feels to me a lot like slamming into that glass barrier at the airport. Having filled my lungs in the oxygen-rich atmosphere of Genesis 1, where God casts his expansive vision for his daughters as his image bearers, it is a little disconcerting to turn the page and hit a wall in Genesis 2, where God's grand and glorious vision for his daughters seems suddenly to shrink. The second chapter of Genesis gives a more detailed account of God's creation of the woman, but the world seems smaller here. There doesn't seem to be as much oxygen in the air as I first thought.

Genesis 2 is where the description of the woman narrows from that of image bearer to "helpmeet" (thanks to King James);[4] from woman as ruling and subduing the whole earth to woman as wife, mother, and homemaker; from being a leader to being a follower; from a breathtaking global vista for women to a concentrated focus on marriage and family. As a wife and mother myself, I value deeply these significant callings and am personally convinced that even in the church we have underrated the seriousness of these callings. But here's the problem. If God is casting the mold for all women when he creates Eve and defining his purposes for all women, as Christians have traditionally supposed, and if that mold only involves her being a wife and mother, then all of us —*including* wives and mothers—are in deep weeds.

That point was driven home for me unexpectedly when my family gathered in Oregon to celebrate my parents' sixty-fifth wedding anniversary, and my brothers and I produced a list of statistics from sixty-five years of marriage that sounds a little like stanzas from *The Twelve Days of Christmas*: 4 kids, 8 grandkids, 9 great-grandkids, 5 pastorates, 12 moves, 1 cat, 3 goldfish, 5 dogs, a multitude of hamsters, and a parakeet (but no pear tree as I recall).

None of these statistics surprised us. What did surprise me was to see on paper the fact that out of sixty-five years together, only thirty-three were with kids at home (which is certainly well above the average). For thirty-two years and counting it has just been the two of them. If we include the years from the day my mother was born until she married my dad, she's been on active duty as a mom for *less than half of her life*. What is more, ten years ago debilitating pain took my mother out of the traditional role of a wife she so beautifully fulfilled for most of her adult life and sent my dad into the kitchen.

Here are a few more numbers to ponder. According to 2009 data from the U.S. Census Bureau, 50 percent of American women fifteen years and older are married and 5 percent of them are separated. If you include girls under fifteen, then the number of married females drops to 40 percent. So for the church to concentrate its primary message for women on marriage means the church is communicating a message that does not strictly apply to approximately 60 percent of women and girls in the pews.[5] To define women solely in terms of marriage and motherhood simply does not fit the reality of most of our lives. Even for those women who enthusiastically embrace marriage and motherhood as their highest calling, a substantial part of their lives is without a husband and/ or children, as my mother's history proves. Furthermore, the traditional message to women is tenuous at best—all it takes is a single tragic phone call for her to be dropped from that demographic. It happens every day.

Add to this the crying need for the church to speak with potency and purpose into the lives of young girls who are drowning in enticing messages that tell them their value resides in the shape of their bodies, their sexual attractiveness to guys, and their wardrobe, popularity, and other fleeting allures. A message that points to the marriage altar as the starting gate of God's calling for women leaves us with nothing to tell them except that God's purpose for them is *not* here and now, but somewhere down the road.

A message of purity and abstinence, as important as this is for young women (as well as for young men), comes too late for huge numbers of young American girls—around 70 percent of them, including many Christians—who by the age of eighteen have had sex at least once and not always by choice. A purity message is utterly devastating to the one in four women who by eighteen has been sexually abused. Women who struggle with sexual identity, who march to the beat of a different drummer, who choose not to marry or have children, whose marriages don't and will never fit the "norm" no matter how hard they try, or who have been ravaged by abuse, violence, and trafficking are left without a place—*as women*—in God's Story.

Considering the numbers and the real lives these statistics represent, shouldn't we be asking more penetrating questions about God's calling for women? For example, do the answers we embrace fully address the many changing seasons, circumstances, callings, and giftedness of our lives? Is it possible for some women to finish the job God created them to do long before their lives are over or, even worse, to entirely miss God's main purpose for creating them? Are we putting little girls and young women on hold until they marry and have children? What if they don't marry or can't bear children? Is it possible that at any moment some unexpected tragedy or misstep can downshift our lives from significance to the margins of meaninglessness? Are God's purposes for women that fragile? Was an older divorced friend of mine right when she murmured dismally, "I had my chance and I blew it"? Is the Bible's message inadequate for women and girls in the twenty-first century, or are God's purposes for us bigger and far more dynamic than we ever imagined? Does the gospel's redemptive message open the door for every woman and girl to be an active, contributing member of the body of Christ, or are some of us beyond hope?

HUMAN RELATIONS 101

Genesis 2 is not out of sync with Genesis 1. Nor is the Bible's opening chapter a rough draft that God tosses out to start over with a scaled-down vision when he sculpts the first woman into being. The larger vision he is casting in the beginning remains firmly in place. Genesis 1 draws our attention *vertically* to the foundational and utterly vital bond between women and God by revealing our image-bearer calling. Everything about us depends on a solid link with God. For both men and women, this relationship alone completes us, defines our identity, and gives our whole lives meaning and purpose. Genesis 2 focuses us *horizontally* on the second most foundational relationship in all creation—the relationship between male and female. Once again, we're eavesdropping on God, who is thinking out loud as the biblical camera zooms in on the creation of male and female, and God defines the nature of their relationship.

God created the man out of earth and placed him in the garden. Then suddenly and rather dramatically, for the first time in the creation narrative God is not pleased. There's a problem in Eden, and God both names and solves it. "It is not good for the man to be alone. I will make an *ezer kenegdo* for him." These two statements are crucial to our understanding of God's design for male and female relationships and deserve our close attention.

God's methods are poetic, mysterious, and instructive. God could easily have taken another fistful of earth to create the woman. Instead, he creates the *ezer* from Adam's body—by taking "a rib" from Adam while he was in a deep sleep. This translation is somewhat misleading. A closer rendering indicates that "*God took a good portion of Adam's side.*"[6] Hebrew scholars think Adam's "side" is more accurate than Adam's "rib," which actually corresponds much better with Adam's later reaction to the woman: "This is bone of my bones *and* flesh of my flesh; she shall be called 'woman,' for she was taken out of man" (Genesis 2:23; emphasis added).

Not only does this signify a profoundly intimate connection between male and female (which the man immediately acknowledges), but God's method for creating Eve also carries beautiful redemptive overtones. The whole human race, beginning with Eve, comes from Adam's wounded side. A second race—a new redeemed humanity—comes from Jesus' wounded side. Jesus is the second Adam. Even before there is despair, God foreshadows hope. The creation of the woman is a sacred, holy moment.

If you follow the math, clearly God is working out something extraordinary. *Oneness* is the preeminent theme. Male and female begin as one, for God forms the woman from the man's side. From one, male and female become two distinct individuals. "She is not a mere extension of man; she possesses a unique individuality in her own right."[7] But the trajectory of their relationship will return them to oneness. From one to two and back to one again.

The oneness God envisions doesn't erase individuality, but actually benefits from and is enriched by their differences. But the oneness for which they are created doesn't leave God out; rather, it finds its center in him. What unleashes the kingdom potency and the enormous good of this male/female oneness is when, like an astronomical syzygy where gravity pulls three celestial bodies into a straight line, the two of them align with God.

In an aside to the reader, the narrator concludes the account by explaining how God's calculus for male/female relationships relates to marriage. This is the first mention of marriage in the entire account. "Therefore a man leaves his father and his mother and clings to his wife, and they become one flesh" (Genesis 2:24 NRSV). This radically upside-down statement would have shocked the original readers of Genesis and should shock us too. I don't know of any culture where men are depicted as clinging to their wives.[8] Certainly within a patriarchal world, this is getting things backwards. There the wife leaves her parents and is absorbed into her husband's family.

This mention of marriage is not to say marriage is for everyone, but to communicate that in God's eyes the ultimate objective of marriage is oneness so that despite their uniqueness and differences, husband and wife are united — "one flesh." This is God's ideal for marriage — an objective profoundly complicated and sometimes beyond reach because of our fallenness. But oneness of this profoundly deep nature between male and female is not the exclusive domain of marriage.

ALONE

Surprisingly little attention is given to what God says about the man. Some commentaries and articles skip right over this part and head straight for the discussion of the *ezer*. Yet anyone reading the creation Story for the first time would be jolted to hear God say, "It is not good for the man to be alone." Ironically, if we take seriously what God is saying here, men run into the same dilemma women encounter. Taken at face value, God's statement actually stirs up some awkward issues for men — some that thin the oxygen for them too.

If Genesis 2 is the creation of marriage, home, and family, and if God is casting the mold for men as well as women, the point seems to be that every man needs a wife. Scholars have gone on record making that precise point: "It is not good for a man *to live alone without a wife* [emphasis added]."[9] If this is what God means, shouldn't we be teaching men and boys that a man's highest calling and greatest fulfillment is to be a husband and a father (and probably also a gardener too)? I've heard sermons guiding men to be better husbands and fathers. Not once have I heard anyone tell men fulfillment of their manhood hinges on having a wife and fathering children, although the same logic produces that kind of message to women. Given how we apply this passage to women, I find it ironic that men don't name "husband and father" first on their résumés. Instead, men define themselves by their occupations.

But if God is making a blanket statement that applies to all males and covers their whole lives (including but not confined to marriage), then all of us have some serious rethinking to do with regard to relationships between men and women. God doesn't specify when or where or under what circumstances it is not good for the man to be alone. This begs the question: In what sense was the man alone?

ONE OF A KIND

When the man awakens in a brand new world with endless discoveries to make and so much to explore, it is not surprising to find him unaware that something important is missing. To impress on the man the importance of the *ezer*, God brings the animals for Adam to name. Lest anyone think the man was flawed, bear in mind that the man is God's creative masterpiece—a work of genius and a marvel to behold—for he is fearfully and wonderful made. He isn't portrayed as lonely, depressed, hungry, bewildered, inept, or crying himself to sleep at night. The task of naming the animals required intelligence, analysis, creativity, stamina, and probably a lot of patience. Illustrations in children's books fail to capture the complicated challenge of Adam's assignment. Natural science museums give a better sense. Zoologists trace the origins of their field of scientific research to this moment. But in naming the animals, Adam comes to realize he is alone—a word that means "to be separate and isolated."[10] No one else exists who is just like him, and now he feels it.

Surrounded by animals in the Garden, Adam was hardly *physically* alone. Furthermore, he uniquely enjoyed a sin-free relationship with God and was the sole focus of God's attention, which must have been incredibly satisfying. Still, Adam was profoundly alone in at least two significant ways. He was, after all, the only human being on earth. He had no peer—no one like himself. First, he was *alone in his relationship with God*. No other creature on earth was called to live by faith. And as we've already noted, trusting God has never been easy. Imagine doing that alone. Second, Adam was *alone in his mission* to be God's image bearer and to build his kingdom on earth.

Animals are a significant labor source. But no one shared the burdens with Adam or worked beside him at the personal level. There was no one to strategize, dream, or plan with him. As I noted in *Lost Women of the Bible,* with the overwhelming global mission God was about to unveil, "the potential for overload, burnout, discouragement, and unbelief was enormous, worse considering the fierce opposition the Enemy was about to mount."[11] God knew the man needed someone to join him in the walk of faith, to shoulder the burdens of the mission, engage in the struggles, watch his back, and stand with him against the Enemy. God had the perfect answer in mind.

But there's a much deeper layer of aloneness we haven't yet touched that gets to the heart of why the man's aloneness was so significant for God. The most glaring aspect of Adam's aloneness centers on his image-bearer calling. Adam is one. But the God he represents is trinitarian—*three in one*. A solitary image bearer is missing a key component of God's image and is therefore incapable of revealing God in the world, much less fulfilling his destiny as a human being. Little wonder God says, "It is not good for the man to be alone."

The Trinity is a mystery no one can adequately explain. So while it's interesting to speculate on parallels between the Trinity and relationships between men and women, we are only on solid ground when we focus on what we know for certain. Stanley Grenz gives us the facts. "God is one. God is three. God is a diversity. God is a unity."[12] One God, but three distinct persons, who delight in self-giving love and rich mutual fellowship, are perfectly aligned in purpose and work together as one. God's vision for humanity is for us to embody this same "oneness in diversity."

This means more than that we should "get along" with one another. Much deeper issues are at stake. When God looks at the earth—as though peering in a mirror—he wants to see himself reflected back. And the place he wants to see the clearest reflection is in his image bearers—both as *individuals*, but more importantly, in our *relationships*. That clearly seems to be what Jesus had in mind when he prayed for all of them "that they will all be one, just as you and I are one—*as you are in me, Father, and I am in you*" (John 17:21, emphasis added). This is utterly profound, for it means God is entrusting his reputation to our male/female relationships. We are telling the world what God is like by how we interact, value one another, build his kingdom together, and move towards trinitarian oneness.

This exposes the appalling state of affairs. It is not merely that God's image is desecrated where violence and atrocities are rampant as we saw in the previous chapters, but also in the more polite and religiously approved forms of division, dysfunction, and the tense negotiations over roles and rank that are widespread among believers in marriage, the church, and every other place our paths cross.

The simplest solution we've devised so far has been for men and women to divide and work separately. It's not hard to imagine what God must think of that. In Genesis God is multiplying the mystery of the Trinity in his image bearers by creating another individual who stands on level ground with the man and is completely different from, yet one with, him. The oxygen hasn't grown thin after all. God is still vision casting—this time for male/female relationships.

THE *EZER-KENEGDO*

My first serious encounter with my calling as an *ezer* happened in the middle of the night. It was around 3:00 a.m., and it changed my life. I wasn't tossing and turning in bed, but wide awake, pouring over books, smuggling volumes out of my husband's study, and searching for answers. I felt like a detective and I knew I was onto something. For years I had been troubled by interpretations of Eve that left me and a lot of other women out in the cold. I was looking for answers, but I was not at all braced for what I was about to find.

God could have given any number of labels to the woman. He chose *ezer*, which in English Bibles is translated "helper." *Kenegdo* is translated "suitable" or, as in older English translations, "meet," which (as I discussed in endnote 4) explains how we ended up with "helpmeet." This in turn has led to interpretations of the woman as the man's assistant, wife, mother of his children, and manager of their home, which as we've noted excludes some 60 percent of females in this country alone. How many millions of women and girls are we leaving out worldwide?

Focus on the wife as her husband's helper has led to the belief that God gave primary roles and responsibilities to men, and secondary, supporting roles to women. It has led to practices that communicate that women are second class citizens at home and in the church. None of this is true. There is nothing second class about God's vision for his daughters, and the *ezer* holds the clues.

For starters, *kenegdo* needs rehabilitating. "Suitable" can be taken a lot of different ways that don't do justice to the meaning of this word. *Kenegdo* indicates the *ezer* is the man's match—literally, "as in front of him"[13]—as Ying is to Yang. I love how Victor Hamilton puts it: "[*Kenegdo*] suggests that what God creates for Adam will correspond to him. Thus the new creation will be neither a superior nor an inferior, but an equal. The creation of this helper will form *one-half of a polarity and will be to man as the South Pole is to the North Pole*" (emphasis added).[14] She will be his strongest ally in pursing God's purposes and his first roadblock when he veers off course.

Long before I started digging, scholars tallied up the twenty-one times *ezer* appears in the Old Testament: twice in Genesis for the woman (Genesis 2:18, 20), three times for nations to whom Israel appealed for military aid (Isaiah 30:5; Ezekiel 12:14; Daniel 11:34), and here's the kicker—sixteen times for God as Israel's helper (Exodus 18:4; Deuteronomy 33:7, 26, 29; Psalms 20:2; 33:20; 70:5; 89:19 [translated "strength" in the NIV]; 115:9, 10, 11; 121:1–2; 124:8; 146:5; Hosea 13:9). This last piece of information created quite a stir as you might imagine, prompting the upgrading of *ezer* from mere "helper" to "*strong* helper." What followed was a divided (and at times heated) discussion over the meaning of "strong"—How strong is strong (a debate yet to be resolved)?

I decided to look up each of the twenty-one references. What caught my attention—and completely changed how I think of myself—was when I read all those verses and discovered *ezer* is used consistently in a military context. Israel seeks military aid from her neighbors. God is his people's "shield and defense," "better than chariots and horses," standing "sentry watch over his people."

Remarkably, even Eden fits this pattern, for although some may balk at the thought, it is fair to say that even the idyllic garden of Eden was a war zone. The command to rule and subdue put God's image bearers on high alert that fierce resistance lay ahead. God commanded the man to keep, or guard, the garden[15] by using the same military language later used for the cherubim who guarded the garden with a flaming sword—a primeval light saber—after Adam and Eve are evicted (Genesis 3:24). The reason, of course, is that a powerful Enemy is already plotting an attack.

Putting the facts together, isn't it obvious that the *ezer* is a warrior? And don't we already know this in our bones? God created his daughters to be *ezer*-warriors with our brothers. He deploys the *ezer* to break the man's aloneness by soldiering with him wholeheartedly and at full strength for God's gracious kingdom. The man needs everything she brings to their global mission.

Other factors confirmed my conclusions. Of course, the strength God brings as *ezer* to his people should be sufficient to convince us that as *ezers* we must be strong, resourceful, alert to the cries of the needy and oppressed, and proactive too. Support for the *ezer*-warrior comes from other Bible passages that use military language for women. Both Ruth and the Proverbs 31 woman are called women of valor (*ḥayil*). Paul rallies believers, both men and women, to "put on all of God's armor" (Ephesians 6:10–17) in preparation to do battle with the Evil One, reminding us that our battle is "not … against flesh-and-blood enemies" (Ephesians 6:12). Thinking of the *ezer* as a warrior is entirely consistent with how Scripture views us.

Reading through one of those tedious genealogies (passages we tend to skim when reading through the Bible), I spotted *ezer* again ... in men's names! Believe it or not, men in biblical times were called Eli-*ezer*, Abi-*ezer*, and just plain *Ezer*. Don't you think it's odd that Jewish fathers would name their sons *Ezer*, especially since this word applies to women? Even more odd considering Hebrew parents gave names to inspire, not to embarrass their children.

Even in recent history, evidence is strong that the name *Ezer* still carries a lot of weight. *Ezer* Weizman (1924–2005), a tall, colorful, larger-than-life figure, was an Israeli military hero. He built an international reputation as a fighter pilot, commander of the Israeli Air Force, a world leader involved in Middle East peace negotiations, and Israel's seventh president. I doubt if anyone made fun of a man like that because his parents named him *Ezer*.

Descriptions of the woman as dependent, needy, vulnerable, deferential, helpless, leaderless, or weak are—to put it simply—wrong. Such definitions betray cultural biases and I fear a deep-seated misogyny. The *ezer* is a warrior. Like the man, she is also God's creative masterpiece—a work of genius and a marvel to behold—for she is fearfully and wonderfully made. The *ezer* never sheds her image-bearer identity. Not here. Not ever. God defines who she is and how she is to live in his world. That never changes. The image-bearer responsibilities to reflect God to the world and to rule and subdue on his behalf still rest on her shoulders too.

God didn't create the woman to bring half of herself to his global commission or to minimize herself when the man is around. The fanfare over her is overblown if God was only planning for her to do for the man things he was perfectly capable of doing for himself or didn't even need. The man won't starve without her. In the garden, he really doesn't need someone to do laundry, pick up after him, or manage his home. If Adam must think, decide, protect, and provide for the woman, she actually becomes a burden on him—not much help when you think about it. The kind of help the man needs demands full deployment of her strength, her gifts, and the best she has to offer. His life will change for the better because of what she contributes to his life. Together they will daily prove in countless and surprising ways that two are always better than one.

THIS CHANGES EVERYTHING

This changes everything for women and girls! God deploys his daughters—all of us—to be *ezer*-warriors for his kingdom all the days of our lives. As a daughter, I love the idea that we are to follow in our Father's strong *ezer* footsteps by soldiering alongside our brothers for his kingdom. A name like *ezer* gives women and girls a lot to live up to no matter who we are or where we live. We have a message for women —big enough for all of us, sturdy enough to survive the worst situations, and generic enough to frame our stories in any season, culture, epoch, anywhere in the world.

The real question facing women is how to fortify ourselves for the daunting mission God has given us. Surprising as it may sound, the *ezer*-warrior's first line of defense and her primary source of strength is her theology—what she knows about God. The life of faith is hard. Even the strongest among us will not be spared dark nights of the soul. We are foolish to think we can stand firm ourselves, much less offer strength to others if we have armed ourselves with cotton candy theology. God gave us minds and he means for us to use them. We need to know God better, so we won't be trying to trust a stranger when the lights go out and we're in a spiritual free-fall.[16] Abundant resources are available today, and seminary doors are open to women to help us on our way.

This changes everything for men! According to God, "It is not good for the man to be alone." This problem is significant enough for God to bring the wheels of his creative activity to a grinding halt and to raise the alarm. God created the perfect solution—the *ezer-kenegdo*. The most significant *ezer* in a man's life is his wife. Surely this ought to transform how Christian men view and value women and girls. Surely it ought to transform what men consider when choosing a wife and how a husband regards his wife—not as dependent, but as a strong and indispensible ally who shares with him the battles and the burdens of life.

In God's family, brothers need their sisters. Even in the church it is not good for the man to be alone. According to Genesis 2, God never intended for men to try to survive without the spiritual ministries of women. He never intended for men to do the work of the church *alone* without their sisters. Most men, if they stop to think about it, can name *ezers*—mothers, wives, sisters in Christ—God has used in their lives to influence, inspire, guide, teach, and strengthen them in their walk with God.

Although neither Jesus nor Paul ever married, both counted on the wisdom and ministries of *ezers* for wisdom, strength, and encouragement. Jesus' mother, Mary, was a valiant *ezer* when she was just a young teenager. No one will forget her courageous self-sacrificing abandonment to God's purposes when he summoned her to duty. Mary was Jesus' first teacher and mentor. Moreover, as the hour of his death approached and Jesus was most alone, an *ezer* from Bethany stood with him, affirmed his mission, and ministered powerfully to him by anointing him for his burial. Jesus said, "She has done a beautiful thing to me" (Mathew 26:10; Mark

14:6). God guided Paul to a band of *ezers* in Philippi, who partnered with him in planting the Philippian church (the first Christian church in Europe) and became an unstoppable and deeply needed source of courage and support for the unmarried apostle. They weren't the only ones, if Romans 16 means anything.[17]

The question facing men is how they will avail themselves of the *ezer*-allies God has provided. Even the secular world is beginning to recognize the extraordinary potential for richer discussions, eliminating blind spots, and making better decisions when men and women work together. After the 2008 Wall Street meltdown, some analysts were wondering if the world economy would be in the same mess if Lehman Brothers had been Lehman Brothers *and Sisters* instead. In 2009, the executive managing editor at *Forbes Woman*, Mary Ellen Egan, reported a growing consensus among business leaders that more women "would have balanced out some of the decisions" and that "you need both men and women in positions of power to really make things work properly."[18] What sounds like a new and revolutionary idea is as old as the garden of Eden—not simply that women should be given a place at the table, but rather that things improve and better decisions are reached when men and women work together.

After humanity's departure from Eden, relationships between men and women started to unravel. Instead of battling the Enemy, we battle each other, and women are reduced to supporting roles. Is God's vision for his daughters a lost relic from the distant past, or is it still alive and well today? Two brides—both ideals, one in the Old Testament and one in the New—show us that God has never abandoned his vision for his daughters. Together they send us an unmistakable signal that God still expects much of his *ezers*.

DISCUSSION QUESTIONS

1. What parts of your life get left out when the *ezer* is defined exclusively in terms of a wife and mother?

2. What reaction did you have the first time you learned that God is an *ezer*? How did it change your self-perception to realize you are an *ezer* too?

3. Why is it "not good for the man to be alone"?

4. How is every woman an *ezer*-warrior for her whole life, married or not?

5. How does it change everything for the *ezer* to be a warrior? How does it make a difference for you?

CHAPTER 6

HERE COMES THE BRIDE!

It was her wedding day, and she wanted to set fire to her wedding dress.

The aspiring arsonist was a prepubescent child bride in Yemen fighting for her life. Reem Al Numery was twelve when her father forced her to marry her thirty-year-old cousin. She told U.S. Embassy officials, "While my hair was styled for the ceremony, I thought of ways to set fire to my wedding dress. When I protested, my dad gagged me and tied me up. After the wedding, I tried to kill myself twice."[1] Her cousin—so-called "husband"—beat and raped her to consummate the marriage.

Other dire consequences accompany child marriage. Traditionally in Yemen, marriage brings the curtain down on a girl's education, stunting her intellectual development, sentencing her to be a perpetual child and dependent to her educated husband, and squandering her priceless God-given gifts and potential. Furthermore, the child bride joins a high-risk demographic, for a girl under fifteen is *five times* more likely to die in childbirth than women in their twenties.

Trauma and suffering are multilayered for child brides (some as young as eight) when a father sells his daughter into the hands of an older man and walks away counting his money, relieved at having successfully offloaded the economic burden of a daughter. The level of betrayal is hair-raising when the man who should be her first line of defense against abuse is complicit in the evil perpetrated against her. It sends a devastating message of her value that she can hardly miss.

Pitted against the combined strength of two grown men, Reem's story is all the more remarkable. Physically, legally, and culturally, the men held all the cards. She was utterly alone. Yet a fearless tenacity and an unbreakable defiance (to the point of preferring death to submitting to such conditions) won her freedom. Details are scarce, but it seems her suicide attempts were serious enough to warrant court intervention. Her story and those of other child brides have ignited the international community to exert pressure on behalf of other Yemeni girls who have been sold into early marriage.

BRIDE SEARCH

Are things really different on this side of the globe? A professor at a well-known Christian college expressed his concern that the number one quality young men on campus were looking for in the women they dated was *submissiveness*. Having seen the promise of the smart, gifted, and high-achieving women in his classes over the years, the professor was disturbed that instead of being valued for their God-given strengths and potential, these young women were expected to pretend to be less than themselves in relationships with men. By prizing a woman's readiness to give in, young men were setting up a scenario that promoted selfishness in them and deprived both parties of authentic relationships.

The professor was also alarmed at the potential for abuse,

which tragically is compounded when a woman doesn't know how to stand her ground. Statistics from many studies indicate that on any given Sunday, approximately one out of four women in the pews are being or have been victims of verbal or physical abuse.[2] Frankly, I'm not sure in this day and age parents want to be setting their daughters' default mode to "Yes."

Cause for alarm is magnified in wider evangelical circles when female godliness is simply or primarily defined as submissiveness, surrender, and meekness. These are important Christian attributes that we see in Jesus, but it is *always* problematic to pick and choose a subset of attributes instead of embracing the full range of qualities Jesus displayed. The problem is worsened if we assign cultural definitions to these Christian attributes instead of letting Jesus define our terms.

Jesus' definition of submission isn't about *giving in* to the whims and wishes of others. It is rather about *giving out* from the completeness we have in him and our passion for his kingdom. The submission Jesus models is gospel centered, for he was aligning himself with God's purposes and pouring himself out to rescue a lost humanity (Philippians 2:3–9). Submission for us follows that same trajectory of putting the interests of others ahead of ourselves, and we trivialize this attribute when we reduce it to a tiebreaker over which shade of paint to use for the guest room. Jesus' brand of submission demands extraordinary levels of tenacity, strength, and courage.

Making "submission" the operative word for women takes on a chilling aura when we factor in young girls like Reem. What would have become of her and the countless other Yemini girls if she had embraced submission as her primary mode of operation? Teachings that Christian women in the West embrace are not only irrelevant in some situations; they are actually dangerous and will certainly cost lives. And while we may not have child marriages in the West, there are still plenty of situations here where a girl or woman is frighteningly at risk and won't be doing anyone good if the only attribute in her arsenal is submission.

One of the powerful stories in *Half the Sky* is of a young Indian Muslim girl who was sold to sex traffickers when she was eight or nine.[3] Five months before her first period, Meena was taken to a brothel where she (like Reem) proved so recalcitrant that her captors beat, drugged, and raped her into submission. Twice she became pregnant. Her children were taken from her to become the next generation of victims. Yet no matter what brothel owners did to her, Meena never lost her will to fight. "Her distinguishing characteristic is obstinacy. She can be dogged and mulish.... She breaches the pattern of femininity in rural India by talking back — and fighting back."[4] And when you read her story, you're cheering her all the way. Meena eventually freed herself and was reunited with her children. Her son, Vivik, helped free his sister. It was said of him that he "inherited his mother's incomprehension of surrender."[5]

Are Reem and Meena allowable exceptions given their extreme circumstances, but for the rest of us, their kind of behavior is out of line? Are we defining a "wartime ethic" for women where, in certain situations (life and death, for example, or in the event the men are absent) heavy lifting, strong leadership, and assertiveness are permissible, but are otherwise unnecessary, unnatural, and unacceptable? If Reem and Meena became Christians, would they be in for a major overhaul to eliminate their stubborn tendencies, or would we celebrate them as exemplary *ezers*, hold them up to our daughters for inspiration, and talk about them to our sons as the kind of courageous woman they should seek for a wife?

At the heart of this discussion is the very real question of whether the gospel's message for women is merely a kinder, gentler version of the world's message. Are we only dealing with a sliding scale, where our beliefs move women to a safer, more acceptable zone of human value, or does Jesus bulldoze that system and reconstruct in its place a radically different *gospel* way of valuing women? Does the gospel's countercultural message *only* overturn degrading cultures like those of Reem and Meena, or does it *also* overturn our own more civilized but equally fallen culture by leading us back to God's original vision for humanity? Are we even asking questions like this? Are we right to think we've figured out how God means for us to live as his image bearers because we don't sell our daughters, or do we have blind spots too and lots more ground to gain? Do our teachings, and more significantly our practices, measure up to the gospel's view of women, or are we selling Jesus and his gospel short because we aren't fully valuing and mobilizing half the church?

STRONG *EZER* ROLE MODELS

The Bible has no shortage of strong, courageous *ezers* with whom Reem and Meena have much in common and who challenge our views of ourselves. Israel's first and only female judge, Deborah—the Sandra Day O'Connor of her day— wisely led the nation and settled their disputes. She summoned Barak into a battle of ridiculous David-Goliath odds against the formidable forces of Sisera and his nine hundred iron chariots and didn't flinch when Barak insisted she go too. The David-Goliath odds for Jael, an ordinary home- maker, were laughably hopeless compared to what David and

Barak faced. That didn't stop her. Armed only with a bowl of milk, a blanket, and a tent peg, Jael with the stealth of an undercover agent and the power of the Lord, finished off the invincible Sisera. Deborah and Barak paid tribute to her as "most blessed" of women (Judges 5:24).

Rahab the Canaanite prostitute, a notorious Jericho traitor, risked her life to harbor Israelite spies and to embrace their God. She saved her family. Abigail subverted her husband Nabal's wickedness by shrewdly appeasing an armed and dangerous David, thus preventing needless bloodshed. Esther overcame her well-honed skill at submitting to confront the two most powerful men in the world, and in doing so rescued a nation from genocide. Mary of Nazareth risked enormous personal disgrace, the threat of abuse and honor killing for bringing shame on the family, and almost certain poverty to give birth to Jesus and save the world.

The Bible doesn't look askance at any of these women, but to the contrary acknowledges God's hand on their lives and reveres them for their faith, strength, and bold activism. Why is it that no matter how many strong, heroic *ezer* stories we find in our Bibles (and there are plenty more), we are never called to this kind of bold proactive living? It seems to be more than a little ironic that with this amazing line-up, the attributes these women exhibit seldom appear on checklists of men who are in search of a wife. As one man sheepishly admitted, "Men generally feel threatened by the strength of a woman. If she is weaker and dependent, that makes it easier for him to lead."

This kind of thinking is difficult to sustain in light of God's creation vision for women and for men. It is significantly undermined by two well-known brides in the Bible—one in the Old Testament and one in the New—whose husbands delight in and are blessed by their many achievements.

Ancient and Future Brides

Like the dazzling extravaganza that comes at the end of a fireworks display, the first bride—the widely celebrated Proverbs 31 woman—is the magnificent grand finale of the book of Proverbs, and the second bride—the bride of Christ—appears in a blaze of glory in the final two chapters of the Bible (Revelation 21–22). The first bride's story surfaces in a private conversation between King Lemuel and his mother, who is guiding her son to think carefully before he chooses a bride.[6] Proverbs 31 paints a full-orbed, down-to-earth, deeply human picture of true wisdom living as she moves through the ordinary spheres of life and functions at maximum capacity.

The second bride is revealed in the New Testament, making her official debut at Pentecost in Acts 2 with the coming of the Holy Spirit, who indwells and empowers her. She is the people of God, the followers of Jesus, the church of Jesus Christ. She is a kaleidoscope of diversity of every imaginable variety, a multitude of people bonded together by God's Spirit into one, yet scattered throughout the world. Jesus entrusted her with his Great Commission (an expansion of God's creation mandate) to "go and make disciples of all nations, baptizing them in the name of the Father and the Son and the Holy Spirit. Teach these new disciples to obey all the commands I have given you" (Matthew 28:19–20).

What brings these two brides together in this discussion is the fact that the Bible holds up *both* of them as ideals. Dealing with ideals is a mixed blessing of sorts, for although the first bride is highly regarded in Christian circles as the patron saint of the homemaker and stay-at-home mom, in the minds of many others she creates unrealistic Martha Stewart-esque expectations of women and idealizes domesticity and diminishes other spheres we inhabit. On the flip side, the spotless, unblemished bride of Christ is cause for enormous hope, for as we have daily evidence and are painfully aware, this bride in her present state is anything but perfect. It is hard to argue with the preacher who said, "The bride is ugly." It is heartening, however, to know her future is exceedingly bright, that she will one day be everything Jesus calls her to be.

Given this second bride's significance, it does seem a little odd that she is left out of discussions and sermons about women. She is ignored when subjects are on the table such as Christian marriage, *ezer* callings, or godly virtues that women should embrace and men should prize in them. I find this puzzling. Perhaps part of the problem is the fact that this bride encompasses not just the female half of the church, but also the male half. We are all the bride of Christ. Although this caused one well-known West coast pastor great consternation (he considered it "very bizarre" to think of himself as a bride), this is what Jesus' apostles teach us in the New Testament, and they didn't seem to think it was unmanly. I think including men actually makes this conversation a lot more interesting because for once they are *inside* of the subject with us and compelled *to think of themselves* when they draw conclusions about how women should live.

Both brides deserve a place at the table, *especially because* they represent the ideal. As such, both contribute to that missing chapter in Genesis by filling in lost pieces of God's original vision for us. The Proverbs 31 woman takes us back to Eden and shows us by her wisdom living what Eve never had the chance to do. And the bride of Christ leads us forward to the fulfillment of that vision—where at long last God's image bearers will enjoy that bone-of-my-bones oneness with Jesus that was the promise and hope of Eden and is the trajectory of our lives today. It is time to unleash the powers of Proverbs 31 for all of us and to start living as the bride of Christ.

Into the Time Tunnel

Both brides take us into a time tunnel where we are transported outside our own time and place. The Proverbs 31 bride takes us back in time to an ancient culture completely alien to our twenty-first-century Western world where, despite our romantic notions of wanting to be the next Proverbs 31 woman, probably none of us would want to live. Her world was ancient, agrarian, and patriarchal—a labor-intensive society where everyone worked hard to survive and made everything from scratch, much like people still do today in rural regions of developing countries. No electricity, running water, shopping malls, household appliances, cell phones, Internet, SUVs, or smoothly-paved superhighways. Visiting her world, you can be sure we'd miss the modern conveniences of home. And while this surely means we are stretching things to think the purpose of her story is to shore up a twentieth-century American way of life completely unknown to her, her cultural background is an important vehicle to get her timeless message across.

The bride of Christ is a New Testament, first-century image drawn largely from within the Greco-Roman world. So she too is introduced in a time and place where patriarchy defined the social structure. In the household—which was both family, home, and business—the man was lord and master of his children, his slaves, and also his wife, who on average would be considerably younger than her husband and certainly not in any sense his peer. But this bride transcends time and place as she lives in every epoch, culture, and location on the planet, and is last seen in the Bible on the edge of eternity.

These two brides are bridges between the lost world of Eden and the coming world where heaven and earth are reunited and God's vision for his image bearers—both his daughters and his sons—is in full force. So what do these brides contribute to our understanding of God's vision for his *ezers*?

LEARNING FROM THE BRIDES

One of the most obvious facts about these brides—and something that ought to give readers whiplash—is that their value is not measured by a patriarchal system of weights and measures. Within patriarchy worldwide, *sons* are the gold standard for assessing a woman's worth. A woman's stock rises exponentially with each additional son she births. Yet in Proverbs 31:28, the mention of sons (usually translated "children" and may also include daughters) comes at the end, not as the *reason* to praise her but as a *source* of the praise she deserves for her wisdom and her deeds. She is valued more than rubies[7] "because she uses her strength, ability, wisdom, and valor so totally and selflessly for others."[8] But the value of the bride of Christ far exceeds even this, for Jesus "[loved] the church … [and] gave up his life for her" (Ephesians 5:25). Both statements are shocking departures from the culture's views of women and give us a potent gospel message for women who are being pulled down by negative messages telegraphed regularly from their cultures.

Both brides inherit the *ezer*-warrior's mantle for they are both called to action. One of the most surprising discoveries resulting from ongoing scholarly excavations in Proverbs 31 is the use of military language throughout to describe this bride's relentless and proactive initiatives on behalf of others. Proverbs 31 belongs to the literary genre of heroic poetry, which is "characterized by recounting the hero's mighty deeds, usually his military exploits."[9] Lyrics praising the Proverbs 31 woman stand alongside the Song of Moses and Miriam (Exodus 15) celebrating Yahweh as the mighty warrior who delivered the Israelites from the Egyptians, the Song of Deborah and Barak (Judges 5) after defeating Sisera's army, the songs that women sang lauding the victories of Saul and David (1 Samuel 18:6–7), and David's tribute of lament to the fallen King Saul and Jonathan and in praise of their military feats (2 Samuel 1:17–27).

The Proverbs 31 woman is introduced as a "woman *ḥayil*"—the same Hebrew word used for Boaz and signifies "strength" and "power" like that of an "elite warrior similar to the hero of the Homeric epic."[10] The meaning, however, gets lost in translation, for whenever *ḥayil* applies to a woman in the Bible,[11] translators have opted for softer English words ("virtuous," "excellent," "capable," or "noble character"). These words don't begin to do justice to the meaning, for in reality *"it may well be that a woman of this caliber had all the attributes of her male counterpart."*[12] She is a woman of valor—an apt description of an *ezer*.

The rest of the poem is drenched in powerful military language, which underscores her *ezer*-warrior calling and reveals her as a force to be reckoned with for all the right reasons. Almost every verse underscores her self-assured confidence and vast capabilities. Unfortunately, even here our English translations bury the strength of the language. The best translations reveal that

> she is "valiant" (31:10), like a conqueror gaining plunder (31:11), a nocturnal predator making the kill (31:15), a "taker" of land (31:16), "girding her loins" with strength, with powerful arms (31:17), supporting the community like a king (31:9, 20), fearless (31:21,25), astute in business dealings (31:18, 24), counseling wisdom (31:26), and

publicly praised in the city (31:31). She provides materially for her household (31:11–4, 18, 21, 27) and earns fame for her man (31:23).[13]

Stated in contemporary language, she is a renaissance woman of sorts—a savvy businesswoman, an employer, strategic thinker, an entrepreneur, profit-making investor, philanthropist, and a forward thinker, to name a few. According to Bruce Waltke, "Like a conqueror who derides his enemy ... she laughs at her metaphorical enemy, the coming day ... with all its possible alarming prospects or circumstances."[14] Part of what makes this bride so significant is that she doesn't simply feather her own nest but moves beyond the boundaries of family and home and uses her resources and wealth to benefit the poor and the oppressed.

Military language is also used in addressing the bride of Christ—not as a call to militancy or harshness, but to arm her for combat with the Enemy, who ever since Eden has engaged in open warfare against God and his image bearers and now does battle with Jesus' bride. Paul tells the bride in Ephesians 6:10–12 that her enemies are "*not* ... flesh and blood [emphasis added]," but the unseen spiritual forces of evil and darkness. She is called to arm herself for battle, to "be strong in the Lord and in his mighty power," and to "stand firm"—all of which convey "unflinching courage like that possessed by soldiers who determinedly refuse to leave their posts irrespective of how severely the battle rages."[15]

Both brides represent an unmistakable call to action. They give us powerful feminine images of strong, open-throttled living for God's kingdom, which makes it difficult to imagine that God wants his daughters to sit on the sidelines while our brothers do kingdom work without us. Both brides show us what it looks like for a woman to love the Lord her God with all her heart and all her soul and all her mind and all her strength and to love her neighbor as herself. Both brides are summoned and honored for giving 100 percent of themselves to the purposes of God. It is through the vigorous efforts of the bride of Christ that "God will announce to the wider world that he is indeed its wise, loving, and just creator; that through Jesus he has defeated the powers that corrupt and enslave it; and that by his Spirit he is at work to heal and renew it."[16]

Proverbs 31 Man

When the Proverbs 31 woman finally emerged in full-blown Technicolor, a few scholars began to voice concern for her husband. Was she leaving him in the dust? And isn't this the unspoken fear—that a strong, competent, bread-winning wife will diminish her husband and cause him to look bad or withdraw? Does the Proverbs 31 man become superfluous if his wife takes care of everything? It's that old teeter-totter mentality that tells us if women are thriving, men pay a price, and vice versa.

It has been said that "a woman's face is her husband's résumé." According to Proverbs 31, the man stands taller in the community because of his valiant wife. Her joyful flourishing and significant community-wide endeavors are a positive reflection on him. He relies on her wisdom—not simply in managing her own widening spheres of influence, but as his best sounding board and wisest advisor. "She brings him good, not harm, all the days of her life.... She speaks with wisdom, and faithful instruction is on her tongue" (31:12, 26). Their combined efforts mean kingdom work is multiplied. Far from being shamed in the city gates,[17] her husband is regarded with greater esteem because he has such a wife. And he is first to sing her praises.

When the apostle John sees the final vision of the Lamb and the bride in Revelation 21, the bride is revealed in all her glory, but what he describes isn't what you might expect. What the angel reveals to John is not a beautiful, marriageable young woman but the new Jerusalem, coming down out of heaven. The new Jerusalem that descends to earth from heaven is nothing other than the church. John is dazzled by her beauty and uses jewels and precious stones to describe the image he sees. Simon Kistemaker eloquently describes the bride:

> This church portrayed here as the holy city Jerusalem is filled with glory. The city itself has no source of light but depends for its brilliance on the glory of God. Just as the sun beams its light to the moon, which in turn reflects the light of the sun, so God's glory illumines the church, which in turn diffuses the light.[18]

TALL DAUGHTERS, MORE CATTLE

While writing this chapter, a friend emailed me another bride story written by Jeffrey Fleishman for the *Los Angeles Times*. The article, "Tall Daughters, More Cattle," was about Sudanese fathers who trade their daughters as brides in exchange for cattle. "Tall girls fetch more cattle because their daughters will quickly grow and can be married off to fetch even more cattle," the local chieftain explained. "A tall girl can command 60 to 100 cattle from a suitor. A short girl may get 20 head, and, sometimes, short girls overstay their welcome in the father's home and end up fetching only five cattle. By then, a tall girl has already borne five children." When Fleishman asked what the women thought of these arrangements, the chief replied, "Women have no say."

Every time I read or hear a story like this—and lately there seem to be a lot of them—I have an overwhelming sense of frustration that we are not trumpeting to the world a stronger message for women. We have a message! It's big enough for all of us and better than any other message out there. In God's eyes, women are not pawns for trading, brides for consuming, bodies to traffic, or passive spectators. They are his image bearers. They are his *ezers*. That Jesus was willing to die for his daughters tells us how much he truly values us.

God calls his daughters to action—not just the rare heroic "exceptions," but every one of us. He wants 100 percent. Nothing less. That's what it means to love him with all our hearts and all our souls and all our minds and all our strength and to love our neighbor as ourselves. And there is the reality (and I am confident the Proverbs 31 man would back me on this) that our brothers need us to live this fully and that they will be the first to benefit if we do. For what God said in the beginning is as true today as ever: "It is not good for the man to be alone" (Genesis 2:18). We will see that point made even more emphatically as we recapture another missing piece from God's creation vision for us—his key kingdom strategy for his sons and daughters to serve him together as a "Blessed Alliance."

DISCUSSION QUESTIONS

1. What is your reaction to Reem's story, and what character strengths did she need to escape from her husband?

2. How are the two ideal brides discussed in this chapter important to our understanding of what it means to be an *ezer*?

3. How does the military language in Proverbs 31 change your opinion of the ideal bride portrayed there?

4. What does Jesus expect from his bride, and how does that impact how you see yourself as an *ezer*-warrior?

5. How does being an *ezer*-warrior change the way you see yourself, and how does this equip us all to live our lives no matter what circumstances we face?

CHAPTER 7

THE BLESSED ALLIANCE

"I would die for this!"

One of the deepest joys of my work is seeing women get serious about pursuing deeper relationships with God as his image bearers. And I absolutely love telling women God created them to be *ezer*-warriors. It's not a hard sell, believe me. At the most basic level, women already know this about themselves. Women are fighting battles all the time—for their families, loved ones, and colleagues; for their faith; for some struggling soul they've taken under their wing; for important community causes; or for some out-of-their-comfort-zone project God has summoned them to do.

I won't soon forget the fire of excitement in the eyes of a great-grandmother who told me, "I thought I was finished. I was going to sit back and enjoy my grandkids. But God has more for me to do!" Young girls come alive when they understand God's purpose for them is *now*, not somewhere down the road. But the part of God's original design that strikes the deepest chord with women and yet is hardest to swallow is the part about the Blessed Alliance between men and women. In a world of dysfunctional and embattled male/female relationships, this part of God's vision for women seems more like fantasy than something within reach, and yet there are few things we desire more. Upon hearing that she was an *ezer*-warrior called to this Blessed Alliance, one young woman declared: "I would die for this!"

DIVINE DESIGN

I've often wondered if our best worship leaders shouldn't be coming from the scientific community. When scientists investigate the endless frontiers of creation—probing upward in the universe and downward into the microscopic intricacies of the atom and DNA—it makes sense that they would be the first to fall on their knees with songs of praise to the Creator, whose wisdom envisioned, planned, and created such marvels. The legendary sufferer Job wasn't a scientist, but that's exactly how he responded when God took him on a nature walk. Somehow, contemplating God's creation and how beautifully it all works together under his all-seeing eye reminds us that our God is a Master Architect who knows what he is doing, even when his ways are baffling to us. This is why we must continue pouring over those blueprints—the ones he spread out in the opening chapters of the Bible.

At creation, God was implementing his vision for the world and for us. Nothing was haphazard. Everything was by design. At the same time he introduced strategies for how he means for things to work—strategies that are directly connected to who he is and reflect his character. Abandoning those strategies is not simply less efficient; it means his glory is diminished in the earth, for we reflect his image most clearly when we do things his way.

His divine design reveals his desire for the kind of intimate parent-child relationship with his children that we long for in our human families, whether we're the parent or the child. Like a proud parent, he envisioned taking pleasure in seeing us launch out boldly on the grand adventure he had in store for us, delighting in our relentless curiosity as we explore the world he created and put to use the good gifts he planted inside us. He anticipated the satisfaction of giving a hearty "Well done!" to each of his children at the end of our journeys. I can only imagine how much it meant to both the Father and the Son when the Father spoke his "I am well pleased" at the beginning of Jesus' earthly ministry.

God also envisioned his sons and daughters forging a Blessed Alliance that would become an unstoppable force for good in this world. We know this because when he created his male and female image bearers, Genesis tells us "God blessed them" and then spread before them the global mandate to rule and subdue on his behalf. Like the owner of a cosmic family business, God deployed his sons and daughters to fulfill his good purposes throughout the earth. In a sense, the cross isn't the only vulnerable moment for God, for at creation he is vulnerable too—lavishing a world on us, giving us the place of highest honor in his heart, and setting us free to make the most of it—with every intention of looking on our efforts together like a proud Father. Instead, we rebelled and went our own way.

Today, the Blessed Alliance seems hopelessly beyond our reach. It may surprise some readers to learn that in my conversations with women, including women seminarians and leaders in ministry and business, by far and away the dominant issue is how we can build bridges with our Christian brothers. Topics like women's ordination, debated Pauline passages, and equality between men and women fade into the background next to this one. I haven't conducted an official survey, but from what I've observed there's a deep desire among Christian women to serve God, heart and soul, with their Christian brothers. Yet, in the church—even in some of the best situations — male/female relationships are the source of some of our biggest hurts, conflicts, misunderstandings, and tensions on both sides.

It's a problem as old as the human race and frankly seems insurmountable at times. History, culture, and entrenched ways of relating to members of the opposite sex go against us. I'm not an expert on male/female relationships, although after growing up with three brothers and being married to a Texan for thirty years, I suppose I should be. But I struggle with this along with everyone else. I've felt the tension. I've heard the fears. I still wince when I recall an objection raised by a pastor years ago: "If we work with women, won't we be tempted?" The battle of the sexes doesn't stop at the church doors, but comes right on in. Yet despite the size and duration of the problem, hope remains alive because the Blessed Alliance matters to God. It is his divine design.

LOAD-BEARING WALLS

You don't have to be an engineer or a building contractor to know that some walls are more important than others. Do-it-yourself home renovators learn the hard way not to tamper with load-bearing walls. Pull out the load bearing walls, and you'll bring the roof down. So before you start demolition on a home improvement project, make sure you know which are the load-bearing walls and leave them alone.

God designed the world to stand on two load-bearing walls. The first load bearing wall is God's relationship with his image bearers. Without this vital relationship, we are cut off from our life supply — homeless, stranded souls in the universe, left to guess at who we are and why we are here. The second load-bearing wall is the Blessed Alliance between male and female. According to Genesis, male/female relationships aren't simply necessary to perpetuate the human race and make life pleasurable and interesting.

Male/female relationships are *strategic*. God laid out his game plan in Genesis, and the team he assembled to do the job was male and female. Men and women working together actually predates men working with men and women working with women. It would be one thing if God confined this male/female team to home and family and then mapped out the remaining territory into separate spheres for men and for women. But he didn't do that. Their mission—*together*—is to rule and subdue the whole earth on his behalf. Men and women together. Our relationships with God and with each other are the load-bearing walls of God's original design.

This foundational truth elevates the seriousness of the Blessed Alliance well beyond men "making room" for women and trying to tweak the system here and there to keep us happy. Much deeper kingdom issues are at stake than resolving debates over disputed passages, deciding who's in charge, resolving conflict, defining his and her roles, and dividing the proverbial pie so everyone gets their fair share. God said, "It is not good for the man to be alone." This statement means our brothers cannot be the men God created them to be or do the job God is calling them to do without their sisters. Together, we are God's preferred method of getting things done in the world. He created his image bearers male and female, blessed them, and spread before them the global mandate to build his kingdom.

A lot is riding on this Blessed Alliance. First, *God's reputation is on the line*. People are supposed to find out what God is like from what they see in us both as individuals and together. It is not going too far to say that we are participants in divine revelation. When male/female relationships in the church are uneasy and distrustful, when we splinter, divide, and cautiously hold one another at arm's length, we are sending false messages to the world of what God is like. When men are called to full-fledged kingdom living but the other half of the church is asked to sit on the sidelines, there is no Blessed Alliance, the bride of Christ limps, and we misrepresent God's oneness.

Second, *our identity and flourishing as human beings hinge on the Blessed Alliance.* God created us to need each other. Male/female relationships are designed to enable us to become our best selves. We'll see hard evidence of this in a moment.

Third, put bluntly — *God's kingdom is at stake.* Carving out a kingdom in a fallen world is our God-given mission. We cannot afford for anyone to hold back. The seriousness of our cause is urgent. Passivity or even a partial effort is unconscionable. The Blessed Alliance is God's strategy for getting the job done. There is surprising God-intended strength and wisdom for all of us when men and women join forces and serve God together. God's purposes for the world are built on these two load-bearing walls.

THE WALLS FALL DOWN

The fall was worse than we thought. The Enemy's first assault was beyond brilliant and wildly successful. With a single temptation — firing one shot — the Enemy targeted *both* load-bearing walls. It was a direct hit. One lethal blow brought down the twin towers of God's kingdom strategy. The Tempter dangled before the man and the woman a shortcut to their image bearer callings — a way to be like God, *without* God. The fast track involved eating the forbidden fruit. No need to bother learning about God and working to be like him. No need to pursue a relationship with God. Suddenly, instead of a Blessed Alliance for God's purposes, male and female were at odds.

Both load-bearing walls collapsed. Dust and rubble were everywhere. Casualties were heavy—100 percent in all. Instead of hungering and thirsting after God, his image bearers were hiding. They severed their lifeline, shattering God's image in them. Instead of repenting and begging to be restored, they began making excuses and passing the blame. Oneness was nonexistent. God's image bearers were divided, and the battle of the sexes commenced. Instead of ruling and subduing the earth, they turned against one another and sought to rule and subdue each other. This was a day of infamy like no other.

Do not imagine God having a stiff upper lip over what had happened to his image bearers and the invasion of the beautiful world he created. Our God grieves over his errant children, just as any parent would do. Grief isn't exclusively a human emotion. God mourns the collapse of the load-bearing walls. The prophet Isaiah described the Messiah as "a man of sorrows" (Isaiah 53:3). We see and hear his sorrow when Jesus weeps over Jerusalem (Luke 19:41) and laments estrangement with his image bearers: "O Jerusalem, Jerusalem, you who kill the prophets and stone those sent to you, how often I have longed to gather your children together as a hen gathers her chicks under her wings, but you were not willing" (Matthew 23:37; Luke 13:34).

Jesus is God's true image bearer. His weeping reassures us that God doesn't keep himself at a safe emotional distance from the sorrows we experience. His heart is bound up with us. He is moved with compassion. He knows how the Story will ultimately end and the heavy cost of the recovery effort. But he enters into our sorrows and weeps with us.

Is there a sense in which we, in our sorrows and broken

dreams, enter into his greater sorrow? When God created the world, he didn't allocate space for cemeteries, hospitals, counseling centers, or legal courts. He created a perfect world. And we have spoiled it and continue to spoil it. According to his original plan, my mountain-climbing brother-in-law Kelly James at 48, Ruth Bell Graham at 87, the stillborn child, the young soldier returning home in a flag-draped coffin—their lives were *all* cut short. So, although God knows exactly what to do and has launched a global rescue operation that will succeed in putting his world to rights and in restoring fellowship with his image bearers, that joyful prospect doesn't negate the enormity of his sorrow now.

When Paul said not "to grieve like … [those] who have no hope" (1 Thessalonians 4:13), he was reassuring us that the sorrow we experience in this world is mingled with the solid hope that sorrow won't have the last word. Somewhere along the line, however, his words have also come to mean that, in some sense, we sorrow *less* than others. Somehow, because of our hope, we are supposed to rise above our losses. Some believe it is a sign of spiritual maturity not to burst into loud sobs at the funeral or to lose sleep over the plight of women in the world. We should smile bravely, hold our heads up high, and show the world the difference faith makes in the face of grief.

I think, instead, perhaps the difference between how we and the world sorrow is that we sorrow *more*, not less, and in our sorrowing we are entering in some mysterious way into God's sorrow. We grieve individual losses, estrangements, prodigals, broken-down lives, the shattered dream; he grieves a world of losses, a world of shattered dreams. We suffer the blinding ache of a parent over a prodigal child; he feels the same ache for a prodigal planet. His is the distress of a master craftsman over a masterpiece destroyed—for the way things are is not the way he meant for them to be. As we grow in likeness to Jesus, we will be gripped by the same sorrow over what is wrong in this world and over our part in it, and we too will weep.

The Enemy's victory could have signaled the end of the Story. But God didn't give up on his vision. Instead of washing his hands of us, God pursued, and continues to pursue, his errant image bearers. Trillion dollar bailouts to rescue a flagging economy are nothing next to what God has expended to recover the Blessed Alliance. God himself is leading the rescue effort. Jesus came to rebuild both load-bearing walls. He is the connecting point between God and us. He is the glue that holds the Alliance of men and women together. He mobilizes his male and female followers *together* to join this rescue effort. Given that fact, it should come as no surprise to discover flashpoints along the way where the Blessed Alliance shines like a beacon in a dark world.

ANCIENT BLESSED ALLIANCES

Two Blessed Alliance examples—one from the Old Testament and one from the New—offer wisdom to the twenty-first-century church. One story comes from the center of Gentile world power; the other from Israel's heartland. The former is the story of cousins—Esther and Mordecai; the latter, a husband and wife—Mary and Joseph. Much like today's Middle East, in their cultures a curtain divides the worlds of men and women. Women embody powerlessness, men command power and authority over women, and relationships between male and female sink to an all-time low. Both women—Esther and Mary—are Jewish and young, unmarried teenagers when we meet them. Puberty has made them marriageable. Both women are immersed in roles their culture assigned. Neither is expecting God to call her out.

Esther and her cousin Mordecai are stragglers who remained in Persia (Iran) after many Jewish exiles returned to Israel. Esther is trafficked—rounded up for the king's harem with all the beautiful young girls—and chosen (after he samples them all) to be his queen. She lives in a world of men—ruled by men. She exists for one man's pleasure. For six years, Esther coasts on standard feminine virtues—beauty and compliance—and stays below the radar regarding her Jewish identity. All the while, her anxious cousin Mordecai (the authority figure in her life) is issuing directives from the sidelines to obedient Esther.

Mary is betrothed to Joseph when she makes her first appearance on the pages of the Bible. Legal arrangements were made between her father and Joseph, and a deal was struck that was as binding as marriage. Money changed hands. She probably knew all her life that she would marry Joseph. She also knew that her primary role in marriage was to bear sons for her husband.

Both stories turn on a crisis that jars everyone out of the status quo. Overnight, existing paradigms for relationships between men and women become unworkable. These crises can *only* be understood within the context of their cultures. Both women's lives are in serious danger because they have committed capital offenses. For Esther, the peril is double. As a Jewess, her life is under threat because a scheme for genocide against the Jews is moving forward. As a wife, her life is in danger from her husband. In Persia an edict is in force establishing the rule of men over their wives. By law, unsolicited meetings with the king are punishable by death. She is trapped by cultural conventions, the law, and her own long history of compliance.

Mary has an out-of-wedlock pregnancy and a wild story to go with it. "I know what you're thinking Joseph, but honestly, I didn't do anything wrong." Her pregnancy is an appalling betrayal and an affront to family honor. In a shame-based culture, the immediate threat to Mary was of death, divorce, or being cast out. For both women, the crisis disrupts dynamics between men and women and turns things upside down. There will be no slight tweaking of the way things "normally" work to wriggle out of these jams.

After calling the shots for Esther's whole life, Mordecai calls Esther to risk her life to prevent genocide. She must rescue her people. To do this, she must stand up to the two most powerful men in the world—King Xerxes and his evil prime minister, Haman. To top it off, Mordecai tells Esther "Who knows but that you have come to royal position for such a time as this?" (Esther 4:14). The pressure is on. In an act of unprecedented courage, Esther throws down the gauntlet: "If I perish, I perish" (4:16)—this in anticipation of a conversation with her husband. Drawing on God's strength and everything she's learned from six years as a palace insider, Esther thinks, strategizes, summons courage, and acts. She takes the lead. She commands Mordecai to call the people to pray and fast. And Mordecai obeys.

By the time Mary collides with Joseph, she has already thrown down the gauntlet. She has said, in effect: "I am the Lord's servant, and I am willing to accept whatever he wants. May everything you have said come true" (Luke 1:38). Looking at pretty images on Christmas cards, it's easy to think the problem Mary faces is the awkwardness of telling Joseph, knowing how this will hurt him. But this is to misunderstand her culture. In patriarchal shame-based cultures, a betrothed girl who turns up pregnant is in danger of honor killing, and the person Mary has most to fear is Joseph, for her "actions" have brought shame on him. Her fate is in his hands.

We have only to recall the story of the three girls buried alive in Islamabad to grasp the danger Mary faced. It should send a chill down our spines when Matthew informs us that Joseph "was a righteous man" (Matthew 1:19). That is not good news if Joseph buys into the Pharisees' exacting definition of "righteous." But this is where Mary's story changes, for unlike the Pharisees, Joseph's brand of righteousness foreshadows Jesus, for whom righteousness means doing right before God no matter the cost. *Before* the angel clues Joseph in on what really happened and exonerates Mary, he has already made up his mind to deal privately with Mary instead of publicly vindicating his honor.

I am not sure from our cultural context that we can grasp how radically self-denying this was in Joseph's culture. It was certainly not the "manly" thing to do. Joseph doesn't stop there. When the angel finally corroborates Mary's story, he shuts down his carpenter shop, gets behind Mary's calling, and adapts himself to his wife and God's calling on her life.

THE GLORIES OF THE BLESSED ALLIANCE

I find it intriguing and exasperating at times that the Bible isn't written more like a "how to" book. Wouldn't it be great to turn to the section on "Blessed Alliance" and find instructions for building a Blessed Alliance in our churches, homes, and jobs? Instead, God reveals his vision and then gives us Jesus and a stack of stories and letters from his apostles. We have to work it out—think, wrestle, and with God's help and a lot of trial and error, try to make our way forward. This means we need to study carefully strong examples like these two young women to distill principles that help explain what made their alliances with Mordecai and Joseph so strong. I don't have a formula. But here are a few observations I find helpful from the examples of Esther and Mordecai, Mary and Joseph.

In both stories, *members of the Blessed Alliance are kingdom minded.* The individual parties in each story get caught up in something bigger than themselves. Kingdom mindedness both compels and frees them to set aside their personal agendas to embrace a greater one. The magnitude and seriousness of God's call on their lives outweigh everything else and demand an all-out effort from everyone. God is mobilizing a rescue effort that requires focusing on the ultimate goal. Esther and Mordecai are called to rescue their people from genocide; Mary and Joseph are mobilized to rescue the world from the clutches of the Enemy. Kingdom mindedness centers them on God's purposes and summons forth from everyone a different way of living and different ways of working together.

In both stories, *the Blessed Alliance calls for gospel living,* which means putting the interests of others ahead of your own interests. Gospel living is on display in both of these stories. Lives are being poured out for the sake of others and for a greater cause. This is the gospel. This is the life Jesus modeled. Both Esther and Mary put their lives at risk. God's call pushes them both out of their comfort zones. They must defy the norms of culture and social conditioning to become bold risk takers. Both have terrifying encounters with powerful men. Both know this could cost them their lives. Their actions reflect God's heart for the world and foreshadow Jesus' gospel. What is more, the men are calling the women to live fully for God's calling—opening doors, supporting, facilitating, challenging. No one is demanding equality or even justice for themselves. Equality and justice are serious biblical concepts, but they are not the issue here.

Both men must give up the right to lead. If they don't, they will obstruct God's purposes. So Mordecai and Joseph put their full weight — their male authority and power — behind the women and God's calling on their lives. Joseph uses his male advantages to benefit Mary. I can only imagine what her mission would have been like in that culture without him. Huge role reversals are in both stories. Women take the lead and are the rescuers. The men are counting on the women to step out and succeed. Mordecai's life depends on Esther's leadership. Joseph's salvation depends on Mary's success.

There's no tug-of-war, no discussion of who's the leader and who's the follower. Leadership is everywhere. It is, after all, every image bearer's calling to accept responsibility and take action. All four of them respond. There is no delicate balancing act, no dividing the pie fifty-fifty to make sure everyone gets their fair share. These would have been the wrong questions. Deeper issues are at stake, which call for a different — *gospel* — paradigm and an all-out effort from everyone.

After being on the receiving end of a rescue effort, this makes total sense to me. During those nightmare days in December 2006 when my family was anxiously waiting and praying for rescue workers to find Frank's brother Kelly James on Mount Hood, we didn't care who led the rescue teams. It didn't matter to us one whit whether it was a man or a woman who found and rescued him. We wanted everyone to do everything in his or her power to bring him safely off the mountain.

Perhaps the most surprising observation I've seen is that *the Blessed Alliance results in mutual flourishing.* This isn't a win for the women and a loss for the men. Instead, by working together, all four of these biblical characters flourish to become their best selves. I can't fully explain it. It's just the way God works. Without question the women shine. Scholars marvel at how Esther evolves from a passive, compliant member of the king's harem to a courageous political leader at the apex of world power. And of course, there's worldwide admiration for Mary and her self-sacrificing choice. But the men are flourishing too.

Mordecai was an adept politician in his own right, but he rises to prominence because of Esther. The win for Joseph is more subtle. He's one of the lost men of the Bible because his story gets eclipsed by Mary and Jesus. We've been walking past Joseph's story for years. It should not go unnoticed, however, that the apostle Matthew gives Joseph the Oscar for Best Supporting Actor. He is the lead story in Matthew's gospel for recovering the true definition of "righteousness." Joseph lives out Jesus' gospel *before* Jesus is born.

For the men, there's a tipping point where everything moves well beyond merely making a place for the women at the table; there is a sudden dawning on Mordecai and Joseph that they *need* the women to follow God's calling on their lives. It will be disastrous if the women take a backseat and expect the men to take care of things for them. One wonders what would have happened to Mary and Esther if the men had refused to cheer them on.

God's tactics are counterintuitive to our male-centered world, but therein lies the surprise for the Enemy, for the world, and for us. For when men and women are allied together, richer discussions result in better decisions, the elimination of blind spots, and a greater kingdom force in the world. If you don't believe me, just compare Esther, Mordecai, Mary, and Joseph each operating solo with what they accomplished by working together.

DYING FOR THE BLESSED ALLIANCE

That young woman was only speaking figuratively when she said of the Blessed Alliance, "I would die for this." But the seriousness of this issue couldn't be expressed more powerfully than the fact that Jesus actually did die for this. The Blessed Alliance is good news unlike anything the world has ever seen. Jesus frames the gospel specifically in terms of unity when he prays to the Father, "May they be brought to complete unity to let the world know that you sent me and have loved them even as you have loved me" (John 17:23).

It's hard to fathom the potential impact a true Blessed Alliance of the church could have on our divided, combative, broken world. I can only imagine how jaw-dropping this would be to the women we've been discussing—Tamam, Marika, the battered women of Guinea, Reem, and Meena—and how they would long to be part of what Jesus is doing.

How to move forward from the dysfunctional present to God's vision is the challenge before us. I still don't have a formula. And I have no doubt that the way forward will be messy. I draw courage from the fact that this is God's vision for us, and that he has moved heaven and earth to open the way for us. Jesus has come.

This is all well and good, but there's an elephant in the room. The Blessed Alliance raises lots of questions. It's not as simple as just moving forward. One of the big obstacles standing in our way is an elephantine debate that has commandeered this discussion for years and shows no sign of stopping. So let's talk about the elephant.

DISCUSSION QUESTIONS

1. What is the Blessed Alliance and why is it so important?

2. In both examples of the Blessed Alliance cited in this chapter, what is the overriding concern of all four individuals and how does that free them to do whatever it takes to serve God's purposes?

3. In both examples, how do all four individuals need each other and how do they each step out of traditional roles and expectations for the sake of God's kingdom?

4. In both examples, how do all four individuals flourish as God's image bearers?

5. What can you do to help rebuild both load-bearing walls of God's kingdom?

CHAPTER 8

THE GREAT DEBATE

"Things are not right here."

A woman nervously pulled me aside in the church corridor and spoke those words in hushed tones to prevent being overheard. She was the leader of a thriving women's ministry in an evangelical church that trumpets its complementarian views regarding men and women. And while she wholeheartedly embraced that perspective, at the same time she was deeply troubled and felt compelled to confide that "things are not right here." Much to my surprise, I heard those very same words from an ordained woman in the corridors of a mainline church that flies the egalitarian flag. Yet there it was again—those same troubling words: "Things are not right here."

What is remarkable about these two conversations (and I have had plenty more just like them) is that neither had anything to do with women agitating for higher rank or wanting to overthrow church leadership or to restructure how their particular church is organized. There wasn't the slightest hint of insurrection. Women who disagree with their church's views on women tend to go elsewhere rather than mount what may inevitably prove to be a futile campaign to turn the ship around. Women who stay are deeply committed. They simply want to contribute, to be part of the conversation, to be valued members of the team. They don't want to create a parallel universe in the church for women, but desire instead to be incorporated into the ministries and life of the body of Christ—to be part of a Blessed Alliance living out the gospel together with their brothers.

THE DEBATE ZONE

Since the late twentieth century two polarized groups—complementarians and egalitarians—have defined the evangelical landscape for women, particularly in the West. The debate between the two groups creates a fault line that runs straight through the body of Christ. Evangelical churches, denominations, and individuals have taken sides. It is a cause of profound division among us.

At the individual level, the question "Are you a complementarian or an egalitarian?" has become a litmus test—a modern *shibboleth* to determine whether a woman is orthodox or heretical, safe or dangerous. Women are routinely pressed to declare where their loyalties lie, and when they do declare themselves, it can cause estrangement. Suddenly friends become foes. I cringe every time I'm asked. It feels like passing through an airport security checkpoint, with church security guards trying to find out if I pose a risk to the safety of the church.

Many of you, busy with everyday life, may not be familiar with the great debate, so let me give you a thumbnail sketch of the issues. *Complementarians* believe the Bible establishes male authority over women, making male leadership the biblical standard. According to this view, God calls women to submit to male leadership and take up supportive roles to their husbands and to male leaders in the church. The complementarian jury is split over whether this includes the public sphere. *Egalitarians* believe that leadership is not determined by gender but by the gifting and calling of the Holy Spirit, and that God calls all believers to submit to one another. At the heart of the debate is whether or not God has placed limits on what women can or cannot do in the home and in the church, although the discussion inevitably bleeds into other spheres of life.

What gives me heartburn about this debate is the fact that after decades of careful study, highly respected evangelical scholars can't agree. These are godly men and women who hold firmly to orthodox Christianity and stand shoulder-to-shoulder defending the authority of Scripture. So many volumes have been written on the subject. So many experts disagree. It can be dizzying to think of wading through the arguments or to imagine figuring out the right answer yourself. After all, if scholars can't settle the question once and for all, what hope is there for the rest of us?

This stalemate, at the very least, ought to inject a hefty dose of humility into this discussion. For many women it creates a boatload of uncertainty and anxiety: Are we overusing or underusing our gifts? Are we too independent, too competent, too strong? Or are we too weak, too hesitant, too deferential? Friends I love and scholars I respect are on opposing sides, wrestling with the biblical text and earnestly seeking to figure out what women can or cannot do vis-à-vis men. I've read the scholars on both sides and studied the texts, and I suspect even Solomon with all his wisdom would have a hard time settling this one.

Dr. John Stackhouse, a world-class evangelical scholar and a man who has served time in both camps, arrived at a similar conclusion with what he describes as "paradigm-shaking force." After extensive research on 1 Timothy 2:11–15, a passage he describes as "easily one of the most obscure of the classic passages on this matter," he writes, "I remember quite clearly now—more than twenty years later—putting the book down on my lap and realizing this insight: Nobody could explain this passage."[1] The best scholars (even while tilting to one or the other side of this debate) will tell you these are complex passages[2] and that it's a hermeneutical best practice to build your theological system on clear texts rather than passages that are subject to dispute.

Meanwhile, as the arguing continues, half the church is living in a debate zone, needing to make choices and to move forward with our lives with amber lights flashing caution at every intersection and respected leaders like traffic cops pointing us in opposite directions. No matter which way we turn, someone (probably someone important to us) will disapprove. Believe me, it's not an easy place to be.

It's Complicated

To complicate things further, the terrain before us is difficult to navigate. Within each of the two polarized camps there are a myriad of opinions and shades of interpretation. Consequently, the boundary line for women's permissible activities gets drawn in multiple places *within the same camp*. Even within a single denomination, churches don't agree on where the line should be drawn for women. Within a single organization what women are allowed to do can change as leaders will, from time to time, tighten or loosen restrictions. What is approved in one location is considered taboo in another. What is biblical one day can be declared unbiblical the next, or vice versa. It's hard to maintain your equilibrium, much less make forward progress, when the ground is moving underneath you like that.

Sometimes a woman's personal circumstances make it difficult, if not impossible, for her to live within the bounds of her own commitments. Doors that are open in theory may remain closed in reality. A Methodist leader estimated that within his egalitarian denomination only 13 percent of ordained women secure pastoral positions because most congregations prefer men. In 2009, the Barna Group reported that only 10 percent of senior pastors were women.[3] According to these statistics, not all egalitarians are able to live out their convictions, and the fact of the matter is that most egalitarians attend churches pastored by men. I know egalitarians who choose to belong to complementarian churches because they are in theological agreement on other issues. Is an egalitarian woman doomed to a perpetual state of frustration if her views are being rejected or only embraced in theory? Are her gifts a source of irritation if doors of opportunity in the church don't open to her? Is she biblically obligated to challenge the local status quo or leave?

Conversely, the most firmly committed complementarian can land in a situation where she has no choice but to cross the line and take up what she believes are a man's responsibilities for leadership, protection, and breadwinning. It happens every day when a husband leaves or dies or for some other reason doesn't (or can't) hold up his end of the bargain. Some men are physically or mentally unable to lead. Men lose their jobs every day, and in an economic downturn, anything can happen.

Lots of women never marry and many are single moms. Are these women forced into a man's role? Are they violating their true calling as women, or are they actually fulfilling God's calling for them as *ezers*? Single women are caught in the awful quandary of developing skills and competencies in the secular world that can lower their marketability as prospective brides. Does the necessity of being the follower compel them to reach for the "off" switch when a marriage prospect surfaces or wedding bells ring? Or should they be valued for bringing these strengths to their marriages?

And what about mixed marriages—where husband and wife belong to different sides of the debate? That happens too. A complementarian newlywed told me her egalitarian husband was bewildered over the change that had come over his bride and best friend since their wedding. "I miss you," he told her. When she explained that he was the leader now that they were married, he responded with, "Then if I ask you to bring your full self to this partnership, will you submit and come back?"

What makes navigating life for women even more confusing is the fact that we don't live in a patriarchal culture. The West is egalitarian. Women enjoy the same freedoms, education, career opportunities, and potential for success as men. Yet instead of wrestling with how to live out the gospel in the culture where God has stationed us, we're supposed to wrestle with how to preserve at least some aspects of patriarchy at home and inside church doors although, for obvious reasons, only certain aspects of patriarchy are deemed worth preserving.

We have thrown out polygamy and slavery. Fathers aren't selling their daughters or arranging marriages. We're as deliriously happy over the birth of a daughter as we are a son. The extended family is no longer a reliable safety net for approximately 50 percent of women who are living solo. According to the U.S. Department of Labor, in 2009 nearly 60 percent of women over sixteen were in the labor force. Christian women live a rather schizophrenic existence as we are constantly moving between two worlds, cultivating strengths, abilities, and experience we may need to set aside when we enter the church or head home. In one world our contributions and expertise are welcomed and valued. In the church we are a subject of debate, and our gifts can be problematic, unwelcome, or allowed only limited use.

Word of this ongoing battle (and other disputes in the church) is leaking out to a watching world. This makes an unappealing impression on women outside the church. Instead of being intrigued and drawn by a community where loving one another is the reigning distinctive, they are repelled by all the infighting and the expectation that the world will grow smaller for them when they step inside. The church seems out of touch and irrelevant at points to the normal lives of Western women. A Christian businessman felt the predicament when he was witnessing to a capable female executive at work and finding her remarkably open to the gospel. The dilemma weighing on his mind was, "When do I break the news to her about submission?"

HERE I STAND

From the beginning of my ministry, I made a conscious decision *not* to take a public position on the ordination of women. My focus has been on calling women to go deeper in their relationship with God (instead of trying to subsist spiritually on a light theological diet). My work centers on women in Scripture who are strong female role models of courageous gospel living, and on casting a vision for twenty-first-century women and girls that extends from the cradle to the grave, irrespective of their preferred debate camp. We are God's image bearers, *ezer*-warriors for his gracious kingdom, and full-fledged members of the Blessed Alliance.

From what I can see, women and girls are a rich and largely untapped goldmine—a powerhouse of blessing and gifts for the church, of strength and wisdom for our brothers, and of enormous good for the world. After all, women do hold up half the sky. Taking sides in the debate seemed an unnecessary distraction that would take me off mission and cost me half my audience — something I am unwilling to do. My decision has not been without consequence.

There are those who read my books like Sherlock Holmes in search of that one statement that will reveal which side I'm on. Some complementarians voice "concern" and "suspicion" about me because I don't *renounce* women's ordination. They wrongly assert that I am against wives and mothers — a strange thought to me since I love being a wife and a mother and consider these frontline kingdom callings. Some egalitarian readers feel let down. My conclusions aren't big enough for them because I don't *affirm* women's ordination. After reading one of my books and failing to find the hoped for punch line, one egalitarian blogger wrote, "It has been a long time since I was this disappointed in a book." My decision may have freed me to focus on other vital subjects impacting women's lives, but it hasn't spared me from the repercussions of the debate or from grieving the negative effect it is having on Christian women and men or how it is hindering our God-given mission in the world.

I make no apology for advocating the Blessed Alliance of male and female image bearers. Rich, collaborative, interdependent relationships between God's sons and daughters are vital to both genders and make the body of Christ stronger. The Blessed Alliance fuels the kingdom of God and must not be displaced by an atmosphere of tension, fear, and mistrust.

I don't discount the importance of the questions being raised by the debate. I realize women who choose ministry vocations don't have the option of avoiding this discussion and must sort through the issues for themselves. But sometimes I wonder if we aren't investing inordinate resources and energies on contested passages instead of putting our full weight down on texts that speak to us with unquestioned clarity. Simply beginning with the two greatest commandments—to love God with all of our hearts, minds, souls, and strengths and to love our neighbor as ourselves—widens the horizon for women and men and opens up new gospel possibilities that push us in a different direction than where this debate is taking us.

THE HOUSE IS ON FIRE

Like quarrelling siblings, we are arguing over how to divide a pie so everyone gets their fair share while the neighbor's house is on fire. While the West engages in debate, millions of little girls are being sold as sex slaves in vast regions of the Majority World—often by their fathers—and human trafficking is happening locally, right under our noses. Even as we debate we must remember the global context. This is not merely an intellectual dispute; it is a matter of life and death for millions of women and girls. This is not to avoid or diminish the seriousness of the debate; rather, it is to enlarge it.

Unlike some other theological debates in the church, this debate has faces: the face of women in war-torn and impoverished lands, anonymous faces behind veils, the faces of our mothers and grandmothers, our sisters, friends, daughters, and nieces, the face women see in the mirror. This debate touches real lives and involves real choices with real consequences. The debate itself may take place in an ivory tower—in scholarly disputations, in books, in theological papers, in wranglings over Greek words and a few hotly contested sentences in Paul's letters. But it plays out in our lives and is anything but academic.

This debate has repercussions on how we live for God, how we relate to our neighbors both near and far, and how we connect with our Christian brothers. It affects the valuing of women, the quality of our marriages, and the teachings and behavioral patterns we pass on to our children. It shapes our ideas of what it means to be part of the body of Christ, how we develop and use our gifts, and what Jesus asks of us in fulfilling his mission for the world. None of these is a minor issue. *Every* woman and *every* girl is impacted *every* day, no matter who we are, where we live, or which vocation we choose.

It is one thing to debate these issues within an ideal framework. But the world is not ideal. We have seen the kinds of ongoing suffering women are experiencing and need to ask ourselves what impact this debate might have on them. Is the gospel truly good news for women who live in entrenched patriarchal cultures — behind veils and under burkas and Taliban rule? What is good news to these women if the gospel reinforces men as leaders and women as followers? How bone-chilling does this sound in the ears of women who are being oppressed or who have been caught in the clutches of human trafficking?

For that matter, how are we putting our own daughters at risk if we teach them that the Bible's default message for women is to submit to male authority? (Ask Sapphira what she thinks now about absolute submission to male authority.)[4] Neither side of the debate is okay with abuse, but are we interpreting Scripture rightly when our conclusions create scenarios where abuse can thrive unchecked? Is Jesus' gospel merely a kinder, gentler version of the world's way of doing things, or does the gospel take us to a completely different, long-forgotten way of relating to one another as male and female? When Jesus said, "My kingdom is not of this world," did he include relationships between men and women?

In this debate, we cannot sidestep the issue of justice. God declares in no uncertain terms, "I, the LORD, love justice" (Isaiah 61:8). Because it is an attribute of God, justice is inextricably tied to our image bearer identity. It is an attribute we are to reflect and a responsibility we bear to the world, "for the LORD is a God of justice" (Isaiah 30:18), and "he will not falter or be discouraged till he establishes justice on earth" (Isaiah 42:4). People speak of the "angry God of the Old Testament" without considering *why* he is angry. Yet anyone reading the Old Testament prophets who speak for him will quickly discover that God is outraged by injustice—when the powerful prevail over the powerless and the privileged over the disadvantaged, when his image bearers are, in any way, dishonored.

Just as injustice ignites the blazing hot ire of God, so *every* image bearer is called to share his outrage at the slightest hint of injustice. As followers of Jesus, justice is our business, and we should be among the first to sound the alarm, to mobilize and be highly visible in bring justice to God's world. Sober care must be taken when we engage in debate over women lest we become participants in something that God hates. And the debate itself must not be allowed to distract or deter us from investing ourselves wholly in the greater business of bringing God's gracious, just kingdom to a suffering world. We have a lot of self-reflecting to do and in-house changes to make in this regard, for injustice is present in our ranks.

Neither can we avoid the stewardship of our gifts. When it comes down to it, we will each face Jesus alone, and more than anything we long to hear his hearty "Well done!" People who have dissuaded us from attending seminary or from stepping up or taking a risk when a situation demanded leadership won't be there to help explain the path we chose (although I suspect some of them will have explaining of their own to do). Ultimately we are responsible for our own choices. How we develop and employ the gifts the Holy Spirit has entrusted to us and (especially for those of us in the prosperous West) what we do with the blessings, freedoms, and privileges we enjoy are matters of the gravest consequence to us. More importantly, they are serious matters to God.

We must not forget that it is still "not good for the man to be alone." Men are impoverished and hampered in fulfilling their God-given callings without the honest, full collaboration of their *ezer*-sisters. Kingdom opportunities are missed and suffering spreads because *not ev*eryone is on high alert or accepts responsibility for what is happening in our world. It is not godly to hold back our gifts and to know less (or pretend we know less) so that men can lead. When women bring less of themselves to the task at hand, men are overburdened and we squander our gifts. On both counts we are culpable.

We read in our Bibles that being part of the body of Christ comes with inherent responsibilities to the rest of the body. You don't need a degree in medicine to understand the difference one body part can make in causing the whole body to be healthy or sick, strong or weak. We feel the weight of this. The repercussions are potentially catastrophic for the welfare and mission of the church, for women make up *at least half* of the body.

NOT OF THIS WORLD

From the beginning, the Bible establishes authority and equality as *foundational kingdom concepts.* Authority belongs to

God. As Creator, he has authority over the earth. Jesus told his disciples, "I have been given all authority in heaven and on earth" (Matthew 28:18). He confers a *derived* authority on his male and female image bearers as his coregents — not to rule over each other, but to rule the earth to ensure both welfare and flourishing.

Equality is a foundational truth that extends to every human being and is rooted firmly in our image-bearer identity. The Bible doesn't nuance or debate equality, but sets it in stone. Equality distinguishes the kingdom of God from kingdoms of this world that rank, rate, discriminate, and privilege some human beings over others. No second class rating, no marginalization, oppression, or mistreatment can alter this rock solid truth, for it is grounded in our unchanging God.

Both concepts were distorted by the fall, along with everything else. God's image bearers turned authority and ruling on one another instead of jointly pursuing God's glory for the benefit of all creation. Equality went missing from human relationships as the human race plunged into self-seeking, murder, violence, power, and oppression. Evidence of how far the human race has fallen is rampant in the appalling oppression and violence perpetrated against women throughout the world.

The New Testament restores authority and equality in the teachings of Jesus and the writings of Paul in ways that are truly "not of this world." Jesus did not come to affirm or make slight alterations to the world's way of doing things. He came to rebuild both load-bearing walls — to reconnect a lost and fallen humanity to our Creator and to reestablish the Blessed Alliance between men and women. His construction methods take us down a different, countercultural path.

WHERE AUTHORITY AND EQUALITY CONVERGE

Jesus' male disciples raised the subjects of authority, power, and rank when on two separate occasions they began jockeying for the top positions in his kingdom. First they argued over "which of them was the greatest" (Luke 9:46); later on, ten of them became irritated when James and John beat them to the punch by requesting places of honor when Jesus ushered in his kingdom.[5] Both times, conflict broke out among the disciples right after Jesus bared his heart concerning the suffering and death that awaited him and the sacrificial nature of his kingdom.

Kingdoms are in collision, and the disciples are clueless at how thoroughly out of step they are with Jesus. They are asking the wrong question. The two episodes have "tragic-comic dimensions. Jesus walks ahead in silence on his way to his sacrificial death while his straggling disciples push and shove, trying to establish the order of the procession behind him."[6] Yet instead of delineating the chain of command in his kingdom, Jesus rejects their thinking as alien to his gospel and links their ambitions for authority to the Gentile [pagan] rulers who lord and exercise authority over others. "Not so with you" (Matthew 20:26), Jesus tells them bluntly. Those who follow King Jesus will march to the beat of a different drummer.

Equality between men and women is a different matter. Issues of justice hang on how much we make of it. Jesus firmly and consistently reinforced human equality by spending a lot of time in the margins of society, most notably in relationships with women. He didn't simply bring relief and comfort to the down and out. He engaged, recruited, and mobilized for his kingdom people who didn't count for anything in the eyes of society or of religious leaders. His interactions with women violated patriarchal propriety and repeatedly shocked his disciples.

Women on Jesus' A-list of potential friends and recruits included prostitutes, adulteresses, a shunned Samaritan, insignificant widows, a ceremonially unclean woman, a dead twelve-year-old girl, and demon-possessed women. Jesus regarded them with unheard-of respect and gave them his undivided attention, even (and perhaps deliberately) when men were around. He engaged women publicly in deep theological conversation in a culture where respectable men avoided public conversations with women. He entered their grief by weeping openly with them. He included women among his disciples, welcomed their friendship, forged strong bonds with them, was blessed and fortified by their spiritual ministries, and recruited them as leaders and kingdom builders.

Daniel Brennan, in his provocative book *Sacred Unions, Sacred Passions*, makes the following point in his discussion of Jesus' post-resurrection meeting with Mary Magdalene, whom Jesus had delivered of seven demons.

> There was more happening in this scene than just the affirmative value of a woman becoming the first witness to the resurrected Christ. Yes, in the resurrection, women are no longer the invisible sex. It is that, but it is much more than that. When Christ met Mary in the garden, friendship—not marriage, not family, not community, but male-female friendship—was the first relationship highlighted and attended to by the risen Christ at the dawn of the new creation according to John.[7]

Jesus' actions led his followers away from gender division to the Blessed Alliance between male and female. According to Andy Crouch, "Jesus did not just teach creatively; he lived creatively, and the guardians of the horizons were unsettled by him."[8] Women in today's world—both those who suffer oppression and those who enjoy unprecedented opportunities—would find Jesus' interactions with women irresistible, life-giving, and profoundly healing.

Equality is assumed. But the gospel doesn't stop there. Even equality gets an unexpected gospel twist. It forms the foundation for how we regard one another but, according to Paul, is not the centerpiece of our relationships with one another. It is here that Jesus' conversations with his authority-minded disciples and Paul's guidance regarding equality among believers converge, and a way forward opens up to our full flourishing as image bearers and to the restoration of the Blessed Alliance. Both Jesus and Paul point us to the gospel.

Beyond Authority and Equality

Jesus pulls his disciples back from their expectation of securing positions of authority over others with a radical (!) call to selflessness. Soon they will see Jesus bend down with basin and towel to minister to them. Already Jesus is calling his followers to a life of *bending down* in service to others. In the kingdom of Jesus, aspirations for greatness involve losing rank, not gaining it—to become "least" of all and seeking "to serve" rather than "to be served." To the natural human mind, gaining by losing is counterintuitive. But it is the way of the cross.

To drive home his point, Jesus draws a little child into their circle—a member of first-century society who, along with women and slaves, registered at the bottom of the human honor scale—without status, without power, and with few if any rights.[9] This insignificant child contrasts sharply with the picture of greatness the disciples envisioned for themselves.

Jesus points them to a lifestyle they did not anticipate. But this is the way for those who follow a crucified Lord.

To make sure they grasp his meaning, Jesus points to himself, for he practices what he preaches. He embodies the kind of leadership his followers must seek. According to Jesus, kingdom leadership is achieved, not by right or pedigree or cultural privilege or self-promotion, but by becoming servants who pour themselves out for the sake of others. It is not about gaining power for oneself, but about empowering others. Jesus identifies himself as the servant who "came not to be served but to serve others and to give his life as a ransom for many" (Matthew 20:28; Mark 10:45).

Paul echoes this same selfless kingdom lifestyle in his letter to the Philippian church. He points his readers to Jesus to teach them the radical demands of the gospel and what true image bearing entails. "Do nothing out of selfish ambition or vain conceit, but in humility consider others better than yourselves. Each of you should look not only to your own interests, but also to the interests of the others" (Philippians 2:3–4). Jesus embodies this radical, countercultural ethos, which those who follow him must emulate in their relationships with one another. Jesus "did not consider *equality* with God something to be used to his own advantage [NIV: to be grasped]; rather, he made himself nothing by taking the very nature of a servant" (Philippians 2:6–7 TNIV; emphasis added)—a bending down for others that ultimately led him to the cross.

The gospel places extraordinary demands on the people of God. None of us is naturally inclined to do what Jesus and Paul are advocating. All of us do daily battle with self-interest. Yet whatever power and privileges Jesus' followers possess are gifts to be held loosely and wielded for the care and benefit of others—especially the helpless, the oppressed, the powerless. Jesus so identifies with the poor, the needy, the least, that he becomes one of them. When his followers care for the poor, the needy, the oppressed, in reality they are ministering to Jesus.

Let us not bypass the fact that Jesus doesn't confine his remarks to a small circle of leaders or his correctives merely to the kinds of competitive comparisons, infighting, and power struggles that occur among people at top levels of denominations, churches, and Christian organizations. Jesus is defining *the ethos of his kingdom* and the costly lifestyle of those who follow him. Neither Jesus nor Paul use "servant" as an adjective joined to "Leader" as we do (often with an uppercase "L"), but as an unadorned, stand-alone noun applied to all who are followers of Christ. Jesus' followers are servants.

A lot of people believe the earth will spin off its axis and civilized culture will collapse if men do not maintain their authority over women in the church and the home. Jesus doesn't share that fear. He fearlessly parts ways with the kingdoms of his world by introducing a new kind of leader—men and women who live sacrificially, not selfishly; who openhandedly aid the poor, the suffering, and the oppressed; and who willingly lay down their lives for the good of others. "This surprising reversal of all human ideas of greatness and rank is a practical application of the great commandment of love for one's neighbor ... and a reaffirmation of the call to self-denial which is the precondition for following Jesus."[10]

Indisputable

What has helped me as I continue living in the debate zone is to study the big picture of Scripture—God's vision for us in the beginning that Jesus came to restore. Rather than build my understanding of God's calling for women on disputed Scripture passages, I have focused first on the lives of women in Scripture to see what God actually calls women to do and how they join their believing brothers in recovering God's kingdom vision for the world. These biblical texts are as authoritative as the disputed texts. Then, regardless of which camp you're in, the world becomes much bigger. The examples here are merely the tip of the iceberg.

I learn from Eve that I am God's image bearer—an identity that comes with heavy leadership responsibility to speak and act as God's representative in the world. She teaches me to be an *ezer*-warrior for God's kingdom in a Blessed Alliance with my brothers to reclaim territory and people the Enemy holds captive and to build God's kingdom together. *This is indisputable.*

Naomi teaches me that no matter what shape my life is in or how little others may think of me, God never counts me out. Kingdom building is a lifelong occupation, and sometimes God is advancing his kingdom in big ways through the efforts of the least among us. *This is indisputable.*

Through Ruth I hear God's call to take responsibility for the needs around me, to live boldly, take risks, fearlessly initiate solutions, and advocate for others even when it means moving out of my comfort zone to engage and challenge the thinking of those in positions of authority over me. *This is indisputable.*

Hannah reminds me that my theology is important. Her theology shaped a nation, instructed kings, and guides believers today. *This is indisputable.*

Mary and Martha challenge me to sit at the feet of Jesus, to learn all I can about him and his Word, to go to seminary if I can, to wrestle and ask the hard questions when bad things happen, and to step out boldly in ministry to others, including men. *This is indisputable.*

Both Esther and Mary remind me that God created men and women to need each other. Allied with Mordecai and Joseph, they displayed the kingdom potency of the Blessed Alliance. Their stories instruct me to be strong and courageous and do my part. *This is indisputable.*

Jesus sobers me with his parable of the talents. It's a serious matter to Jesus when we bury our gifts and talents in the ground instead of employing and investing them for his kingdom. *This is indisputable.*

Finally, Paul reveals that I am a vital member of the body of Christ, that the whole body needs my gifts and ministries, and that it is hindered if I withhold them. *This is indisputable.*

A friend once told me with a sigh, "This old debate will be with us until Jesus comes." At the rate we're going, she's probably right. But in the meantime, I will seek with all my heart to follow these indisputable truths, and I will not be afraid. There is much work to be done. Earth is emitting a distress signal we cannot ignore. Suffering and injustice are rampant, and they are our business. God has called us. We are ready.

DISCUSSION QUESTIONS

1. Realizing that not everyone feels the impact of this debate, describe how living in this debate zone might create difficulties, fear, and uncertainty for women.

2. How did Jesus and his disciples not see eye-to-eye on the subject of authority?

3. What does Paul want believers to learn about human relationships from Jesus' example?

4. How do the teachings of Jesus and Paul take us beyond authority and equality to a radically different, gospel way of relating to one another?

5. How do the non-negotiables help you to shed your fears and move forward with confidence to serve God with heart and soul and strength and mind?

Waking the Sleeping Giantess

"I must do something about it!"

In 1901 a seven-year-old Indian girl escaped from a Hindu temple. Her widowed mother had dedicated her child to be "married to the gods," which ultimately meant a life of prostitution. The traumatized child, whose hands had been branded with hot irons as punishment for a previous escape, found refuge in the arms of Amy Carmichael. It was a watershed moment for Amy, who recorded her shock at the child's "uninhibited stories of life in the temple ... for they revealed a state of things which few missionaries suspected.... Investigations not only confirmed [the child's story], but unveiled an evil greater in its extent and more grievously unholy in its character than ... ever imagined."[1] On the spot, Amy Carmichael made up her mind. *"Since these things are so, I must do something about it!"* [2]

One little girl's escape launched a fifty-year career in intercepting and retrieving girls and babies from a "life" worse than death and giving them a home. It eventually led Amy and her associates to discover little boys being trafficked too and to expand their rescue efforts to include them. She led a band of *ezers* who with her often risked physical danger to defend those who were powerless to defend themselves. Her efforts changed the lives of hundreds of little girls and raised up a generation of believers who were once hopelessly locked in the Hindu caste system.

Amy Carmichael's determined *ezer*-spirit is alive and well today. I was in a bustling Memphis restaurant having lunch with my friend Jacky. She was explaining how, at the Synergy2007 Conference in Orlando, Dr. Diane Langberg's message about sex trafficking had gripped her heart. On the spot Jacky made up her mind. *She was going to do something about it.* Given the magnitude, complexity, and dangers of the problem, the thought of one lone *ezer* making the slightest dent in the crisis sounded unrealistic to me. I was about to learn *never* to underestimate what God and one *ezer* can do.

After the conference Jacky returned home to rally the women in her denomination who were already voicing a determination to impact hard places in the world with the gospel of Jesus Christ. She invited Diane to speak to them. More *ezers* signed up. Jacky led her team to join forces with missionaries and Eagles' Wings Foundation to fund and sustain a transition home in Albania for orphaned adolescent girls who, at the age of fourteen, are forced to leave state-run facilities. Suddenly put out on their own, these girls are open prey for waiting traffickers. The home is licensed to house up to eight girls and is staffed with a social worker, psychologist, doctor, teacher, and home parent. By *preempting* the work of traffickers, Jacky and her team of *ezers* are giving girls safe haven and a life they never knew was possible. Plans are already underway for six to eight more homes. The world becomes a better place when God's *ezers* dare to think big!

Who says one *ezer* can't make a difference?! So what are the rest of us waiting for?

MILLENNIAL MILESTONE

In the year 2000, we rounded the bend from the twentieth to the twenty-first century and from the second to the third millennium. Few generations live to experience such a pivotal moment in time. And although the world didn't come to an end as some feared it might, developments in the new millennium are racing forward at a breakneck pace that takes one's breath away and puts before us unprecedented opportunities, resources, and challenges. Boston University history professor Richard Landes calculates that "we live at a moment when social, economic, and technological change occur at speeds and with a scope never before seen in the history of mankind, at a time when cultures, religions and lifestyles are rubbing shoulders as never before."[3]

In light of God's global vision for his daughters, we owe it to ourselves, to the church, and to the world to stop and reflect. Now is the time to ask ourselves—both individually and collectively—where we are on track with God's vision both for us and for his world, where we've lost our way, and how we need to change and correct course. Instead of lunging forward to do the same things the same way without thinking, it's time to scan the global horizon to see what and where are the greatest challenges and opportunities. Then we must not only get on our knees and pray for God's kingdom to come, but also get up and participate in the answer to our prayers by bringing the promised good news to the poor, binding up the brokenhearted, freeing the captives, and releasing those held captive by the darkness. That is, after all, what *ezers* who follow Jesus are supposed to do.

As for the Blessed Alliance, judging by the state of relationships between men and women, we have obvious reasons to reassess. If the body of Christ were subjected to a millennial physical, would we get a clean bill of health or be rushed into intensive care because only half of the body is fully functioning? Is Jesus' whole body thriving and stronger than ever today because for over two millennia "the *whole* body, joined and held together by *every* supporting ligament, grows and builds itself up in love, as *each* part does its work" (Ephesians 4:16 NIV, emphasis added)? Do the world's headlines read, "See how they love one another!" — not of tight-knit homogeneous subgroups of Christians, but of a bone-deep oneness that inexplicably thrives within wide-ranging diversity and denominational and theological differences and reaches across the gender divide?

In two thousand years, how far have we come in attaining that kaleidoscopic trinitarian oneness Jesus longs to see? How is God's reputation in the world enhanced because of us? Has the world changed for the better, is the Enemy in retreat, and is justice flourishing in the earth because the Blessed Alliance of men and women is formidable and fully deployed for God's kingdom? How is that Blessed Alliance coming along anyway?

SIGNS OF THE TIMES

Astronomer John Mosley commented for MSNBC on theories that might explain the phenomenon of the Christmas star that lit up the skies to announce the good news that Jesus had come. In an article entitled "Wondering about the 'Star of Wonder,'" one appealing theory he presented was of "a rare series of planetary groupings" in the years 3 and 2 BC — a conjunction of Venus and Jupiter in the constellation of Leo, near the star Regulus, the "king star."[4] The result was an unusually brilliant glow in the skies that to the naked eye looked like a single blazing star. The star signaled a momentous event on earth to those who made it their business to keep an eye out for such a phenomenon. According to Mosley's theory, it caught the attention of eastern Magi and compelled them to load up their camels and travel a great distance in search of a king.

Careful observers of what is happening in the opening years of the third millennium are noticing another rare series of convergences. I am neither an astronomer nor a prophet, but with the naked eye I can see at least three. This multiple convergence is unparalleled. It's the kind of phenomenon that, in the business world, makes entrepreneurs salivate over the possibilities and news watchers perk up in anticipation of breaking news. In the world of astronomy it captivates Magi and sends them packing, ready to travel long distances to find out what it all means. Those who make it their business to keep an eye out for such phenomena will see right away that God is opening to us an unprecedented window of opportunity that is too important to miss.

EZER-CONVERGENCES

The first convergence centers on what is happening with women. Today as never before in history, the polarized worlds of women are intersecting. The world has grown smaller because of advancing technology, inexpensive and open communication, social networking, and the forces of globalization. As one friend mused, "In today's world, nothing is very far away." We've passed the point where the world of prosperity and privilege so many of us enjoy can shield us from the world of privation and atrocities, and there is no turning back.

Never before in the history of the world have so many

women in cultures around the world been so blessed with civil and legal rights and protections, higher education, career opportunities, comfortable homes filled with modern conveniences, unprecedented wealth and earning power, and easy access to communication systems and travel. To be sure there are still serious injustices, but compared to previous generations and to the rest of the world, we in the West are exceedingly blessed.

Never before in the history of the world has the desperate plight of women worldwide been more glaringly cast in the spotlight. It is in our faces and happening every moment in every culture, including our own. This paramount global crisis impacting countless women and girls has been there all along, held back by lack of information, the limitations of earlier systems of communication, and by a simple refusal among Christians to believe those who, like Amy Carmichael, have desperately tried to sound the alarm.

The events of 9/11 burst the dam and revealed the appalling truth of what is happening to our sisters worldwide. We are swamped with information, and there's no stopping it now. I never will forget the first time someone illumined me about realities in the world that were beyond my sheltered existence and the horrible shock I experienced. In the previous century, no matter how hard she tried, Amy Carmichael couldn't get the urgency of this brutal reality to sink in and bother people until they acted. Now we can't escape it. The endless, unrelieved suffering of so many who are unable to deliver themselves is a reality we can no longer ignore.

Since the Twin Towers collapsed, hardly a week goes by without some new wave of horror breaking over us—another vivid reminder that the battle rages on. Even as I write this paragraph, CNN is running a report about Fawzia, an Afghan girl married at sixteen who endured three years of constant beatings at the hands of her husband and in-laws, while her parents refused to intervene despite her increasingly desperate pleas. With no means of escape, "Fawzia finally did what she had threatened to do many times before: she doused herself in cooking fuel and struck a match."[5]

These stories appall and make us long for Jesus to return. But until Jesus comes, the cries of the helpless, the suffering, and the oppressed are falling on our ears. In God's good providence, these two alien worlds have come together—the world of those who prosper far in excess of our needs and who are empowered to make a difference for others, and the world of those whose suffer without hope and whose oppressors ravage, degrade, oppress, imprison, and murder with impunity. This convergence is no accident. God is opening *our* eyes. Privilege and prosperity come with responsibility. God's mandate for us to rule and subdue removes from us the option to turn a blind eye or stand on the sidelines wringing our hands. How much does God want? The Dutch theologian Abraham Kuyper answered that question: "There is not a square inch in the whole domain of our human existence over which Christ, who is Sovereign over *all*, does not cry: 'Mine!' "[6]

God's Spirit is stirring the waters, confronting kingdom-*ezers* with the cries of millions of *ezers* in crisis who have no one to deliver, not nearly enough voices sounding the alarm, and far too few of us in the gospel battle for justice, healing, and hope. Whether we like it or not, God is confronting us with his overarching command to "love your neighbor as yourself" and is compelling us to rethink how we answer the question, "Who is my neighbor?" It's time we made up our minds, as other *ezers* have done, that *we are going to do something!*

A Fragmented Gospel Reunites

The second convergence is the reuniting of a gospel that has been split in half for as long as most of the present generation can remember. Today, we are witnessing what Gary Haugen describes as a "sea change" in Christian mission. The *verbal proclamation* of the gospel and *a gospel ministry of justice* have converged once again—two vital aspects of the gospel that are *inseparable* in the preaching of the prophets and in the teaching and ministry of Jesus.

After decades of infighting among Christians and denominations over which of the two facets to embrace (a prolonged and costly controversy that surely made the Enemy smile), the days of choosing which half of the gospel to embrace are ending. Historic fears of the "social gospel" have been displaced by a fuller, more holistic conception of the gospel. It is no longer sufficient or acceptable to share the love and forgiveness of Jesus without also sharing his justice and compassion in bold and tangible ways.

One of the distinctive and heartening aspects of this long overdue convergence is the rise of a "Justice Generation" that includes many young *ezers* in a groundswell of

> younger Christians who find their hearts beating fast with their Maker's passion for justice, who show little tolerance for a gospel that does not embody Christ's call to serve the oppressed, and who are eager to discover how they can use what God has given them to bring a humble and courageous witness for God's justice into an aching world.[7]

Speaking prophetically, Haugen expects this rising generation will

> fashion a fundamental shift in the ministry of the global

church to "seek justice, rescue the oppressed, defend the orphan, plead for the widow" [Isaiah 1:17 NRSV]. And perhaps most gloriously, they will do so in a way that is quite new for the Western church—in relationships of mutual respect, in shared leadership and in common sacrifice with their brothers and sisters in the developing world, where the gravitational center of the Christian faith is increasingly shifting.[8]

Jesus' gospel ministry took on solidly physical dimensions, and the gospel we proclaim should reflect the same. He was a rabbi. Teaching was his occupation. But his teaching was accompanied by radical acts of compassion and mercy. He fed thousands because "I have compassion for these people.... If I send them home hungry, they will collapse on the way" (Mark 8:2–3). Lepers and other untouchables felt the touch of his hand. He didn't recoil from the touch of prostitutes, and he welcomed the ministries of women with and to himself.

I think of Naomi when I read about Jesus' raising a widow's only son back to life. When asked, "And who is my neighbor?" Jesus directed the questioner's attention beyond his intimate circle of acquaintances to a loathed Samaritan—a complete outsider—and spoke of binding up wounds, providing food and shelter, paying bills, and following up. It ought to teach us something that Jesus' final act of public ministry was to address the needs of a widow, his own mother, whose eldest son was dying before her very eyes.

Jesus didn't give us a small gospel. He gave us a full-orbed gospel with vast dimensions that defy the kinds of precise measurements that make us comfortable. The gospel isn't supposed to be comfortable, for it points us back to a cross. It up-ends all our paradigms and pushes us beyond the confines of self-interest to pour ourselves out for others. Jesus' gospel brings salt and light to a tasteless, dark world. His image bearers are agents of those life-transforming forces.

The whole gospel we are commissioned to spread means double good news to the poor, for we bring justice and mercy and Jesus to them. A partial gospel lacks that power. This is how the kingdom of heaven begins to gain ground and the Enemy is forced to relinquish strongholds of evil once thought impenetrable to kingdom forces. Amy Carmichael would be ecstatic.

THE BLESSED ALLIANCE PREVAILS

The third convergence—the Blessed Alliance of God's sons and daughters—is still a work in progress. More and more Christians are talking about it, and that is welcome news. Here and there we see glimpses of the gospel potency God unleashes when his kingdom-minded sons and daughters band together in common cause. But in the main, the Blessed Alliance has never recovered from the deadly assault that took place in Eden. Instead of an unstoppable force for good and justice in the world and a deadly threat to the Enemy, male-female relationships have been dismantled of power. Instead, they are the butt of jokes, bogged down in endless debate and all sorts of fears in some quarters, and scenes of mind-numbing brutality in others.

But let there be no doubt about it. The convergence of men and women for the kingdom of God is as certain to happen as any two planets in our solar system that are locked in a band of gravitational force are bound to align. No tactic of the Enemy and no entrenched blindness on our part have the power to deter God from seeing his vision for us to completion. God's secret plan has now been revealed to us; it is a plan centered on Christ, designed long ago according to his good pleasure. "And this is his plan: At the right time he *will* bring everything together under the authority of Christ—*everything* in heaven and on earth" (Ephesians 1:10, emphasis added)—*including* his sons and daughters.

Having said that, the seriousness of the issue before us here cannot be overstated, for the Blessed Alliance is central to God's kingdom strategy for the world. Without it we are pursuing kingdom work at a serious disadvantage. The first challenge is to ponder the true nature of the alliance God has in mind. The goals we've settled for—drawing lines, defining roles, establishing quotas, developing methods of conflict resolution, and organizing logistics—may ease things a little, but cannot move us to the ultimate goal. We are merely rearranging the furniture when we need to move to a different house.

The Bible employs radical language to describe the Blessed Alliance that stretches our imaginations and calls for a complete paradigm shift. New Testament teachings expose the fact that the way of relating as male and female that we lost back in Eden looks nothing like anything we see in our world today. To help us see this, Jesus resurrects a form of higher math that originated in Eden, and Paul conducts an anatomy class.

The first mathematical equation in the Bible hints of the kind of radical whole-number living God envisions for his image bearers. When he created the first man and woman and gave them a monumental global mission, he said—"the *two* are united into one" (Genesis 2:24, emphasis added). Notice, not two *halves* equal one so they "complete" one another. Their completion is in God. God isn't working with fractions here, but with two complete image bearers who, when joined in common cause with their Creator, will present to the world the clearest reflection of him and a potent force for good in the world. One plus one equals one.

A calculation like that doesn't compute in our world. Not only do we have trouble pulling it off in our relationships, even modern technology resists it. No calculator or computer—no matter how sophisticated, no matter how many times you try—will ever tell you *one* plus *one* equals *one*.

This higher math has divine origins, for it is trinitarian. *One* Father plus *one* Son plus *one* Spirit equals *one* God. No one has ever been able to explain this. Jesus applies the same mathematical logic to those who follow him. According to his calculations, it doesn't matter how many "ones" you add together or how completely diverse they are from one another, the final sum will always be *one*. Jesus' final prayer for us—his dying wish—was that image bearers who follow him would reflect that same trinitarian calculus—that *"all of them may be one*, Father, just as you are in me and I am in you.... May they be brought to complete unity to let the world know that you sent me and have loved them even as you have loved me" (John 17:21, 23, emphasis added). A lot is riding on the fulfillment to Jesus' prayer, for the state of our oneness actually authenticates (or denies) the divine nature of Jesus and his mission. Our oneness, if you will, leaves DNA evidence that Jesus has been here.

The apostle Paul weighs in on this mathematical discussion with a metaphor that shatters every other paradigm for male/female relationships and exposes our definitions of oneness as wide of the mark. Paul employs the language of anatomy. Believers—male and female—form a body. Not just any body, but the *body of Christ*. This is not news to most Christians, but because we hear it so much, our eyes can glaze over when hearing another sermon about the body of Christ;

this, in turn, makes it easy to miss the radical implications of what Paul is saying.

Let me suggest one way to bring this image to life. Go wander the halls of a hospital, visit the sick and dying, and listen to our wounded veterans returning from Afghanistan and Iraq. They will teach us eye-opening lessons on the priceless value of missing limbs and of how the whole body suffers when body parts and organs shut down or only function partially. Their painful testimony compels us to rethink both our ecclesiology[9] and our anthropology[10] especially in light of the relentless, agonizing, and exhausting efforts war veterans expend to get their broken bodies back to maximum strength and health. We will learn from them how precious and indispensible *every* member of the body is to the whole.

Connecting the dots between what they tell us and how we relate to one another as believers is revealing and sheds new light on the calling and mission of women. Can the body do what it was created to do—can it even survive—if half of the body isn't fully functioning and the rest of the body is deprived of their ministries? What kind of body are we giving Jesus? Doesn't Jesus want a healthy, vigorous body too?

We are living at a pivotal moment. In the new millennium, God is opening a strategic window of opportunity that calls for gospel action. The moment of opportunity is now. The apostles cautioned us about presuming what we can put off until tomorrow. If both halves of the church don't step up and the Blessed Alliance remains wishful thinking, we will squander this moment. Either the window of opportunity will close, or with God's help we will unite as never before. There is no room for triumphalism; there is only hard, painstaking work before us. Even in a fallen world, as long as there is a Holy Spirit, there is hope that we can make strides toward becoming the Alliance God created us to be. And as we do, these three convergences will align, the world will be blessed, and the earthshaking good news that Jesus has come will once again light up the skies.

DOUBLE VISION

We started out in search of God's global vision for his daughters — a vision for women of all times, everywhere, and in all circumstances. The Bible has delivered a vision for God's daughters that is more gloriously expansive and life enriching than we have yet discovered. In the beginning God created a world that belongs to him — a masterpiece in every respect. His pleasure in his handiwork is undisguised. "It is good," we hear him say to himself, again and again.

The climax of his creative activity is the creation of his image bearers — male and female. The only time we hear God say, "It is not good," is when the man is alone — in his relationship with God, in his God-given mission, and in reflecting a trinitarian three-in-oneness. But after God creates the *ezer* out of the man's side — same substance, different essence — he says it again, this time with an exclamation point, "It is *very* good!"

God's image bearers are fearfully and wonderfully made. He invests them uniquely with a capacity to know him and a boundless potential for creativity, curiosity, enterprise, and resourcefulness. His vision is for them, together as a Blessed Alliance, to beam back to heaven the clearest and fullest images of himself. God swings wide the door of access to himself and welcomes them into the privilege of knowing him. That alone is a universe to explore.

Men and women are strategic to God's vision for the world. He entrusts the whole earth to their stewardship. All creation beckons their creative energies and depends on their care. Even the relationship between them holds out challenges and potential, for here they will learn love and sacrifice and the power and beauty of oneness. Their God-given mission demands vigilance, leadership, all they have to offer, and *above all*, a solid connection to their Creator. Conflict will draw them out.

The Bible ends with a vision too. Not on a solemn note of defeat, with a whimper of regret, or with a long list of casualties, but with deafening shouts of celebration and a wedding feast so dazzlingly glorious that the apostle John, who is granted a sneak preview at what is yet to be, is at a loss for words to tell us what he sees. As a writer, I find strange consolation in knowing that even an inspired apostle can have writer's block. John is fishing for the right words, for his earthbound point of view doesn't give him reference points to describe the heavenly vision before him. Overpowered by what he sees, he repeatedly falls on his face and worships. Yet he can give us only muted hints of what is yet in store.

The vision signals a new beginning, God's creation vision fully recaptured—a new heaven and a new earth emancipated from the curse and swept clean of the oppressive power of the Enemy and the powers of darkness. There is as well a remade humanity freed from the downward pull of fallenness and the tears of loss and grief. They are entering a new era of oneness with God and with each other. No wonder they are shouting!

The part of the vision that caused me to do a double take is the description of the bride. I understand that in biblical times the groom commanded the spotlight. That focus is justifiably maintained here, for Jesus is the central figure. But the bride (the people of God) draws John's attention as well, for she is reason to celebrate too. John reports the crowd exuberantly shouting about the bride of the Lamb who "has prepared herself. She has been given the finest of pure white linen to wear." John then adds this aside for the reader's benefit: "Fine linen represents the good deeds of God's holy people" (Revelation 19:6–8).

Like an actress imagining herself standing before the millions of fans to accept the Oscar or the athlete envisioning herself standing atop the winner's rostrum with Olympic gold hung round her neck, we are invited to picture ourselves at the marriage of the Lamb, wearing that fine white linen dress that proclaims the good works we have done to build the Lamb's kingdom.

Some scholarly commentators get noticeably nervous at this point, not about seeing themselves in a wedding dress but about taking things too far another way. They are careful to remind us that the bride doesn't stand here on her own merit, sometimes to the point of stripping her of the honor John is telling us she has earned. Of course the bride wouldn't be here if Jesus hadn't sacrificed himself to redeem her in the first place; we eagerly acknowledge that. But what can we say? There she stands, dazzling in a gleaming white, fine linen gown woven of *her* righteous works. Vera Wang would be sketching images right along with John.

The bride has answered the Lamb's sacrifice of love. She loves him back by spending herself for his cause. They are the Blessed Alliance—the Lamb and the bride. This is no passive bride who merely lives on the receiving end and expects Jesus to take care of everything. She is an *ezer*, after all, who enters the fray for Jesus and gives back with every ounce of her being. See how she loves him with all her heart and soul and strength and mind and loves her neighbor as herself. Her accomplishments bring joy to her groom, and all heaven celebrates her, for God created her for this.

These two visions bracket our world, a world that is a nightmare for so many and can make one vision seem impossible to recapture and the other too distant to imagine. But together these two visions possess the power to spur us forward. The first vision frames our lives and tells us who we are, why we are here, and what our mission is in the present. We are God's image bearers. We are *ezer*-warriors, and our brothers need us. We belong to the Blessed Alliance of those who follow Jesus. The second vision fuels our hopes with the *certainty* that Jesus is going to finish the job and that he enlists our participation in finishing it. The bride reminds us that our efforts make a difference, that heaven keeps score, that anything and everything we do for the kingdom is being woven into the mother of all wedding gowns. To borrow from Joseph's words to Egypt's Pharaoh, "The dreams of Pharaoh are one and the same.... The reason the dream was given ... in two forms is that the matter has been firmly decided by God, and God will do it soon" (Genesis 41:25, 32).

WAKING THE SLEEPING GIANTESS

I knew when I picked up *Half the Sky* I was in for a difficult read. The authors don't spare the reader when they expose the atrocities women and girls are suffering in every culture worldwide. They document in graphic detail just how far the world has strayed from God's original vision for humanity. Their message is uncompromising and comports with the battle cry that burst from a grieving and outraged Amy Carmichael in *Things as They Are*: "I mean it with an intensity I know not how to express, *that ... such unutterable wrong ... in the name of all that is just and all that is merciful should be swept out of the land without a day's delay.*"[11]

But the larger, profoundly disturbing point is made that by discarding, trafficking, oppressing, and destroying her daughters, the world is recklessly self-destructing. Evidence is present in every culture that *the sky is falling* when millions of those whom God created to hold it up are missing. That point is underscored repeatedly by inspiring stories of the significant culture-changing contributions of fiercely determined *ezers* who emerge from the world's darkest pits, not to be cared for but to fight costly battles as advocates for others.

With the barest of resources, these heroic women are creatively starting small businesses, educating their children, changing the quality of life for whole communities, and even becoming a constructive influence to fight terrorism. Today, over one hundred years after Amy Carmichael launched her ministry, the Dohnavur Fellowship is *still* rescuing children who are at risk and would otherwise be trafficked or on the streets. The Dohnavur ministry keeps giving back, for the women leading that work today were among the little ones rescued and raised by that community.[12]

Women do hold up half the sky. We are half the church. If women hold up half the sky, what can half the church accomplish?

When the Japanese bombed Pearl Harbor, Admiral Isoroku Yamamoto is alleged to have said, "I fear all we have done is to awaken a sleeping giant and fill him with a terrible resolve." It was a frightening prospect. There was reason to fear what that giant—angered and outraged—would do.

God is shaking his daughters awake and summoning us to engage. His vision for us is affirming and raises the bar for all of us. We cannot settle for less. We have work to do. There's a kingdom to build, and what we do truly matters. Our compass is fixed on Jesus. We can no longer listen to those who call us to love him with less than all our heart and soul and strength and mind. We may not have titles, position, or power in the eyes of others, but leadership is in our DNA. The call to rule and subdue places kingdom responsibility on our shoulders. Conflict draws us out. And as we answer God's call, our brothers will be first to benefit.

Every morning, as the light of dawn breaks over the planet, countless *ezers*—women and girls—are waking up all over the world. If, as we have seen, one *ezer* can accomplish so much, the potential force for kingdom good and the store-house of gifts and ability that reside in the church's *ezer* population is simply staggering. God's global vision for women unlocks that potency, unleashing an unparalleled message of hope and an endless array of kingdom possibilities that ripple out from home, family, and community to reach untouched places where human suffering and female oppression sink to unimagined lows.

I have a friend who believes when she puts her feet on the floor in the morning, the devil shudders and says, "Oh no! She's awake." If one *ezer* makes the devil tremble, what can a whole army of *ezers* do? Who knows what could happen if we took seriously God's vision for us, and what a difference we could make if *ezers* everywhere were waking up with big creative ideas for how God might use them for his kingdom and boldly taking the lead?

One hundred years from now may it never be said of this generation of *ezers* that we folded our hands and left God's kingdom work to others. May it never be said that we ignored the cries of the helpless and focused on ourselves. Let it instead be said that God used those cries to awaken a sleep-ing giantess and filled her with a terrible resolve—half the church, angered and outraged at the unchecked forces of evil in God's world. That we made up our minds to do something, that our efforts forced the darkness to recede, and that we left the world better off than we found it. May we be remembered as a generation who caught God's vision, faced our fears, and rose up to serve his cause.

DISCUSSION QUESTIONS

1. How does God's vision change how you see your place in God's Story and your place in the world?

2. How does conflict in God's Story—the cries of the helpless, the oppressed, the trafficked, the impoverished—summon you to action?

3. Why are both aspects of the gospel—the verbal proclamation of the gospel and a gospel ministry of justice—necessary and inseparable? Why is one without the other not the whole gospel?

4. Beginning right where you are and with the people who are in your orbit, how are you already doing kingdom work? Where do you see opportunities to do more?

5. If one *ezer* can do so much, what can you do?

NOTES

ACKNOWLEDGMENTS

1. Used by permission. The use of Jessica Goodfellow's poem is not intended as an endorsement of the content of *Half the Church*.

INTRODUCTION: SEEING BEYOND OURSELVES

1. Quotation by Kurt Hahn (1886–1974), a German-born Jewish educator who, because of his fierce criticism of the Nazis, was forced to leave Germany. He emigrated to Scotland, where he continued his career as an educator. He later converted to Christianity and preached in the Church of Scotland.
2. Gail Collins, *When Everything Changed: The Amazing Journey of American Women from 1960 to the Present* (New York: Little, Brown and Company, 2009).
3. Nicholas D. Kristof and Sheryl WuDunn, *Half the Sky: Turning Oppression into Opportunity for Women Worldwide* (New York: Knopf, 2009), 244.
4. Rodney Stark, *The Rise of Christianity* (San Francisco: HarperSanFrancisco, 1996), 84.
5. When God creates the woman, he calls her an "*ezer*" (Genesis 2:18). This concept is fully developed in chapter 5. But for now, suffice it to say, this powerful Hebrew word points to the woman's calling to combat the Enemy and the powers of darkness and to advance the kingdom of God. Amy Carmichael's courageous efforts to rescue children from sex trafficking is a perfect example of an *ezer*-warrior in action.
6. Amy Carmichael, *Things As They Are: Mission Work in Southern India* (London: Morgan and Scott, 1904), 3.
7. Ibid., 4.
8. Frank Houghton, *Amy Carmichael of Dohnavur: The Story of a Lover and Her Beloved* (Fort Washington, PA: Christian Literature Crusade, n.d.), 329–30 (emphasis added).

9. Ibid., 117.

10. Amy Carmichael, *Gold Cord: The Story of a Fellowship* (London, SPCK, 1957), 42.

11. Kristof and WuDunn, *Half the Sky*, xvii.

12. Comment on Luke 8:1–3, from J. C. Ryle, *Expository Thoughts on the Gospels: St. Luke* (New York: R. Carter & Bros., 1860) (www .gracegems.org/Ryle/l08.htm).

CHAPTER 1: GOING GLOBAL

1. Nicholas D. Kristof and Sheryl WuDunn, *Half the Sky: Turning Oppression into Opportunity for Women Worldwide* (New York: Knopf, 2009), xvi.

2. Ibid., xvii.

3. Jim Wallis, *God's Politics: Why the Right Gets It Wrong and the Left Doesn't Get It*, (New York: HarperCollins, 2005), 104.

4. Richard Lacayo, "About Face: An Inside Look at How Women Fared under Taliban Oppression and What the Future Holds for Them Now," *Time* (December 3, 2001), 36.

5. Kristof and WuDunn, *Half the Sky*, xvii.

6. Ibid., 10.

7. Ibid., 11.

8. Ibid., xviii.

CHAPTER 2: IDENTITY THEFT

1. Geraldine Brooks, *Nine Parts of Desire: The Hidden World of Islamic Women* (New York: Anchor Books, 1995), 51.

2. Nicholas D. Kristof and Sheryl WuDunn, *Half the Sky: Turning Oppression into Opportunity for Women Worldwide* (New York: Knopf, 2009), 68.

3. Ibid., xvi.

4. Ibid., 68.

5. Ibid.

6. Ibid.

7. Victor Malarek, *The Natashas: Inside the New Global Sex Trade* (New York: Arcade, 2003), xvi.

8. Stanley J. Grenz, *Theology for the Community of God* (Nashville: Broadman and Holman, 1994), 224.

9. See www.youtube.com/watch?v=UmXlzT1zM5M for Mirren's comments on her role of playing Queen Elizabeth II.

10. Rebecca Murray, "Dame Helen Mirren Discusses 'The Queen' "; see

http://movies.about.com/od/thequeen/a/queen100406.htm (accessed October 2006).

11. Colossians 1:15; Hebrews 1:3.

12. John 13:34; Leviticus 11:44 and 1 Peter 1:16; Ephesians 4:32; Philippians 2:5; Ephesians 4:23–24 (emphasis added in all cases).

CHAPTER 3: BEARING GOD'S IMAGE IN A BROKEN WORLD

1. See www.care.org/features/videogallery.asp#; click on "The Girl Effect."

2. Ofeibea Quist-Arcton, "Guinea Shaken by Wave of Rapes During Crackdown," NPR, *All Things Considered*, October 20, 2009, www.npr.org/templates/story/story.php?storyId=113966999&ps=rs.

3. 1 Peter 4:12.

4. 1 Corinthians 12:7.

5. These are the way the four verbs are translated in the NASB.

6. When Jesus discusses marriage and divorce with his disciples, he speaks of eunuchs. These were men who were physically unable to reproduce or who chose to remain celibate: "Some are born as eunuchs, some have been made eunuchs by others, and some choose not to marry *for the sake of the Kingdom of Heaven*. Let anyone accept this statement who can" (Matthew 19:12, emphasis added). Paul picks up the same theme in his first letter to the Corinthian church:

> An unmarried man is *concerned about the Lord's affairs—how he can please the Lord*. But a married man is concerned about the affairs of this world—how he can please his wife—and his interests are divided. An unmarried woman or virgin is *concerned about the Lord's affairs: Her aim is to be devoted to the Lord in both body and spirit*. But a married woman is concerned about the affairs of this world—how she can please her husband. I am staying this for your own good, not to restrict you, but that you may live in a right way *in undivided devotion to the Lord*. (1 Corinthians 7:32–35, emphasis added).

7. Before the book of Genesis concludes, "fruitful" has already split off from "multiply" and stands alone as Joseph explains why he named his second son "Ephraim," a name derived from "made me fruitful" (see Bruce K. Waltke, *Genesis* [Grand Rapids: Zondervan, 2001], 535).

Old Testament scholar Gordon Wenham thinks that "it is a little surprising that after the birth of just his second son Joseph should speak of being fruitful" (Gordon Wenham, *Genesis 16–50* [Word Biblical Commentary; Dallas: Word, 1994], 398).

Considering the bigger picture—namely, Joseph's meteoric rise from a trafficked slave in an Egyptian prison to second in command to Pharaoh in all of Egypt as well as Joseph's relentless diligence in making the most of every situation—Hebrew scholar Victor P. Hamilton (*The Book of Genesis Chapters 18–50* [New International Commentary on the Old Testament; Grand Rapids: Eerdmans, 1995], 512) offers this explanation:

> In naming his second child *Ephraim* [Joseph] reminds himself that God can turn buffeting into blessing. The place of affliction can become the place of fruitfulness. The fruitfulness to which Joseph alludes refers to more than simply the birth of a son. It must include the opportunity to be the vehicle in the survival of Egypt. If the name of Joseph's first son (Manasseh) focuses on a God who preserves, the name of Joseph's second son (Ephraim) focuses on a God who blesses. [emphasis his]

8. Stanley J. Grenz, *Theology for the Community of God* [Nashville: Broadman and Holman, 1994], 226.

9. Andy Crouch, *Culture Making: Recovering Our Creative Calling* (Downers Grove, IL: InterVarsity Press, 2008), 104.

10. See Gordon Wenham, *Genesis 1–15* (Word Biblical Commentary; Dallas: Word, 1987), 32, who writes:

> Ancient oriental kings were expected to be devoted to the welfare of their subjects, especially the poorest and weakest members of society. By upholding divine principles of law and justice, rulers promoted peace and prosperity for all their subjects. Similarly, mankind is here commissioned to rule nature as a benevolent king, acting as God's representative over them and therefore treating them in the same way as God who created them (Ps 72:12–14).

11. Greg Mortenson and David Oliver Relin, *Three Cups of Tea: One Man's Mission to Promote Peace ... One School at a Time* (New York: Penguin, 2006), 209.

12. Nicholas D. Kristof and Sheryl WuDunn, *Half the Sky: Turning Oppression into Opportunity for Women Worldwide* (New York: Knopf, 2009), xxi.

CHAPTER 4: THE SHAPING OF A LEADER'S SOUL

1. Vanessa Parrilla, "Sati: Virtuous Woman Through Self-Sacrifice," Spring 1999, California State University, Chico; see www.csuchico.edu/~cheinz/syllabi/asst001/spring99/parrilla/parr1.htm

2. Lys Anzia, " 'Nothing to Go Back To'—The Fate of the Widows of

Vrindavan, India," *Women's News Network* (Nov. 5, 2007): http://
womennewsnetwork.net/2007/11/05/nothing-to-go-back-to-the
-fate-of-the-widows-of-vrindavan-india/.

3. Ranjan Roy, "Outcast Hindu Women Find Solace in a Holy Town,"
Associated Press, 1996: http://archive.southcoasttoday.com/
daily/08-96/08-19-96/c01li074.htm.

4. For a fuller treatment of the book of Ruth, see Carolyn Custis James,
The Gospel of Ruth: Loving God Enough to Break the Rules (Grand
Rapids: Zondervan), 2008.

5. Marie C. Wilson, *Closing the Leadership Gap: Add Women Change
Everything* (New York: Penguin, 2007), 85.

6. See R. Laird Harris, Gleason L. Archer Jr., and Bruce K. Waltke, eds.,
Theological Wordbook of the Old Testament (Chicago: Moody Press,
1980), 1:271–72: "The individual designated seems to be the elite
warrior similar to the hero of the Homeric epic, and [was possibly]
... a member of a social class. Although in most contexts his military
prowess was involved, he was wealthy enough to bear special taxes ...
[and] was also to be honorable or reputable."

7. James, *The Gospel of Ruth*, 155.

8. Gary A. Haugen, *Good News about Injustice: A Witness of Courage
in a Hurting World* (Downers Grove, IL: InterVarsity Press, 2009),
211.

9. Carolyn Custis James, *When Life and Beliefs Collide: How Knowing
God Makes a Difference* (Grand Rapids: Zondervan, 2000), 106.

10. Ḥesed is a strong Hebrew word that describes the love of God for his
children. But this is no ordinary brand of love, and the English words
that are used to translate it—"love," "loving-kindness," "mercy,"
etc.—separately or in combination are simply inadequate to describe
it. Ḥesed is a stubbornly loyal, self-giving love that motivates a person
to do voluntarily what no one has a right to expect or ask of them. It
sums up the way God intended for his image bearers to live together
from the beginning. In the Bible, ḥesed is defined by actions, and we
see ḥesed most fully expressed in Jesus. Ḥesed is the gospel lived out.

11. According to ancient Babylonian records, a male harvester's pay for
a day's labor was rarely more than one or two pounds. Ruth has har-
vested the rough equivalent of a half-month's wages or more—a mini-
mum of *fifteen* times what Boaz's harvesters were earning as a fair
day's wage. See Robert J. Hubbard Jr., *The Book of Ruth* (New International Commentary on the Old Testament; Grand Rapids: Eerdmans, 1988), 179.

12. C. S. Lewis, *The Problem of Pain* (New York: MacMillan, 1974), 93.

13. Ruth 2:13

14. Nicholas Kristof and Sheryl WuDunn, *Half the Sky: Turning Oppression into Opportunity for Women Worldwide* (New York: Knopf, 2009), 50, 84.

15. Haugen, *Good News about Injustice*, 87.

16. Here is what Leviticus 25:25 says about the kinsman-redeemer: "If one of your countrymen becomes poor and sells some of his property, his nearest relative is to come and redeem what his countryman has sold." The kinsman-redeemer was to invest his own inheritance to purchase his relative's property. The relative or his heirs could buy back the property, or it would automatically revert to the original owner (or his heirs) in the Year of Jubilee. Ruth's proposal is a high-stakes gamble, for if she remains barren, the kinsman-redeemer doubles his inheritance. If she gives birth to a son, it is a losing investment for the kindman-redeemer because everything goes to her child and his own sons inherit less. Elimelech's nearer kinsman-redeemer walks away from Ruth's proposal because he doesn't want to risk financial ruin. His refusal sheds light on the sacrifice Boaz is willing to make.

17. See Deuteronomy 25:5–9 for the levirate law: "If brothers are living together and one of them dies without a son, his widow must not marry outside the family. Instead, her husband's brother must marry her and fulfill the duties of a brother-in-law. The first son she bears will be counted as the son of dead brother, so that his name will not be blotted out in Israel. However, if the man does not want to marry his brother's wife, she shall go to the town gate and say, 'My husband's brother refuses to carry on his brother's name in Israel; he will not fulfill the duty of a brother-in-law to me.' Then the leaders of his town shall summon him and talk to him. If he persists in saying, 'I do not want to marry her,' his brother's widow shall go up to him in the presence of the elders, take off one of his sandals, spit in his face and say, 'This is what is done to the man who will not build up his brother's family line.'"

    In ancient Israel the family inheritance was always divided by the number of a man's sons *plus one* because the firstborn always received a double share. So a man with two sons divided his inheritance three ways, giving his first born two portions and his second son one. If the eldest son died, the second son stood to inherit everything. If he fathers a son for his deceased brother, his inheritance drops by 66 percent, back down to one-third.

18. Kelly Kapic, *God So Loved, He Gave: Entering the Movement of Divine Generosity* (Grand Rapids: Zondervan, 2010), 199.

19. "Students of the book of Ruth often draw attention to the fact that both Naomi and Boaz repeatedly address Ruth as 'my daughter' [Naomi in Ruth 1:11, 12, 13; 2:2, 22; 3:1; Boaz in 2:8; 3:10, 11]. This has led many to conclude that Boaz is an older man and of the same generation as Naomi and Elimelech" (James, *The Gospel of Ruth*, 151).

20. Henry J. M. Nouwen, *The Wounded Healer: Ministry in Contemporary Society* (New York: Doubleday, 1979), 72.

CHAPTER 5: THE *EZER* UNBOUND

1. Greg Mortenson and David Oliver Relin, *Three Cups of Tea: One Man's Mission to Promote Peace ... One School at a Time* (New York: Penguin, 2006), 205.

2. Ibid., 207.

3. *Ezer* is pronounced with a long "â," so that it rhymes with "râzor."

4. The King James Version of the Bible (1611) rendered the Hebrew *ezer kenegdo* in Genesis 2:18 as "an help [helper] meet [fit or suitable] for him." In 1674, the poet John Dryden hyphenated the two words in the phrase "help-meet for man," taking the expression "help meet" one step closer to becoming an independent word applied mainly to a man's spouse, as Eve to Adam. It was not until the nineteenth century that "helpmeet" emerged as a word in its own right. See *The American Heritage Dictionary of the English Language* (4th ed.; Orlando, FL: Houghton Mifflin, 2009), s.v. "helpmeet."

5. U.S. Census Bureau; American Community Survey, 2009 Summary Tables; generated using American FactFinder; see http://factfinder.census.gov (accessed September 2010).

6. See R. Laird Harris, Gleason L. Archer Jr., and Bruce K. Waltke, eds., *Theological Wordbook of the Old Testament* (Chicago: Moody Press, 1980), 2:768: "God created woman by taking 'a rib' from Adam while he was in a very deep sleep. Conceivably this means that God took a good portion of Adam's side, since the man considers the woman to be 'bone of his bones' and flesh of his flesh (Gen 2:21ff). This picture describes the intimacy between man and woman as they stand equal before God."

7. Ibid.

8. "The verb *forsake* frequently describes Israel's rejection of her covenant relationship with Yahweh.... By contrast, the verb *cling* often designates the maintenances of the covenant relationship.... Thus, to leave father and mother and cling to one's wife means to sever one

loyalty and commence another." Victor P. Hamilton, *The Book of Genesis Chapters 1–17* (New International Commentary on the Old Testament; Grand Rapids: Eerdmans, 1990), 181.

9. Harris, Archer, and Waltke, *Theological Wordbook,* 1:91.

10. Ibid., 1:90.

11. Carolyn Custis James, *Lost Women of the Bible: The Women We Thought We Knew* (Grand Rapids: Zondervan, 2005), 36.

12. Stanley J. Grenz, *Created for Community: Connecting Christian Belief with Christian Living* (Wheaton, IL: BridgePoint, 1996), 44.

13. Victor P. Hamilton, *The Book of Genesis Chapters 1–17* (New International Commentary on the Old Testament; Grand Rapids: Eerdmans, 1990), 175.

14. Ibid.

15. "Then the LORD God took the man and put him into the garden of Eden to cultivate it and keep it" (Genesis 2:15, NASB). Victor Hamilton explains the meaning of "keep": "The basic meaning of this root is 'to exercise great care over,' to the point, if necessary, of guarding.... The same root is used in the next chapter to describe the cherubs who are on guard to prevent access to the tree of life in the garden (Gen. 3:24). The garden is something to be protected more than it is something to be possessed" (ibid., 171).

16. To read more on the importance of theology for women, see Carolyn Custis James, *When Life and Beliefs Collide: How Knowing God Makes a Difference* (Grand Rapids: Zondervan, 2001).

17. For Mary of Bethany's story, see *When Life and Beliefs Collide,* 157–76; for more on Mary of Nazareth and on Paul and the women of Philippi, see *Lost Women of the Bible,* 163–80, 205–21.

18. See http://video.forbes.com/fvn/power-women–09/most-powerful-women-leaders.

CHAPTER 6: HERE COMES THE BRIDE!

1. "2009 International Women of Courage Awardees," U.S. Department of State, Washington, DC, www.state.gov/s/gwi/iwoc/119946.htm (accessed March 6, 2009).

2. Stacey Womack, "Domestic Abuse," in Bev Hislop, *Shepherding Women in Pain* (Chicago: Moody Press, 2010), 213.

3. Nicholas D. Kristof and Sheryl WuDunn, *Half the Sky: Turning Oppression into Opportunity for Women Worldwide* (New York: Knopf, 2009), 3–16.

4. Ibid., 7.

5. Ibid., 13.

6. Hebrew scholars debate whether the acrostic poem about "the valiant wife" (Proverbs 31:10–31) belongs to the first nine verses of the chapter because the two sections differ in form and structure, among other reasons. In his commentary on Proverbs, Bruce Waltke argues convincingly for the unity of the two sections. To read more, see Bruce K. Waltke, *The Book of Proverbs: Chapters 15–31* (New International Commentary on the Old Testament; Grand Rapids: Eerdmans, 2005), 501–3.

7. According to Proverbs 3:13–15, "[wisdom] is more precious than rubies; nothing you desire can compare with her." So in Proverbs 31:10, the poet is saying the same thing about the woman.

8. Waltke, *The Book of Proverbs: Chapters 15–31*, 521.

9. Ibid., 516.

10. R. Laird Harris, Gleason L. Archer Jr., Bruce K. Waltke, eds., *Theological Wordbook of the Old Testament* (Chicago: Moody Press, 1980), 1:271–72.

11. "A worthy [*hayil*] wife is a crown for her husband, but a disgraceful woman is like cancer in his bones" (Proverbs 12:4); "Who can find a virtuous and capable [*hayil*] wife? She is more precious than rubies" (Proverbs 31:10); "There are many virtuous and capable [*hayil*] women in the world, but you surpass them all!" (Proverbs 31:29); "Don't worry about a thing, my daughter. I will do what is necessary, for everyone in town knows you are a virtuous [*hayil*] woman" (Ruth 3:11).

12. Harris, Archer, and Waltke, *Theological Wordbook of the Old Testament*, 1:271–72.

13. Mark D. Futato, *The Book of Psalms*, and George M. Schwab, *The Book of Proverbs* (gen. ed., Philip W. Comfort; Cornerstone Biblical Commentary, vol. 7; Carol Stream, IL: Tyndale, 2009), 661.

14. Waltke, *The Book of Proverbs: Chapters 15–31*, 531–532.

15. Gerald F. Hawthorne, *Philippians* (Word Biblical Commentary; Waco, TX: Word, 1983), 56.

16. N. T. Wright, *Simply Christian: Why Christianity Makes Sense* (San Francisco: HarperSanFrancisco, 2006), 204.

17. "In ancient times, the city gate was not only the point of entry into town ... it was also the heart of the community. The gate was the seat of government and the site of important business transactions, a platform for local dignitaries, a pulpit for prophetic messages, and the hub of local gossip for the entire village. So whenever you hear of someone being praised in the gates (like the legendary woman of Proverbs 31),

the entire community from the top down is honoring them. It's comparable to a New York City ticker tape parade for a national hero or having your name emblazoned on a star inlaid on the sidewalk at Hollywood and Vine. Praise in the gates is high honor indeed" (Carolyn Custis James, *The Gospel of Ruth: Loving God Enough to Break the Rules* [Grand Rapids: Zondervan: 2008], 178).

18. Simon J. Kistemaker, *Revelation* (Grand Rapids: Baker Books, 2001), 563.

CHAPTER 8: THE GREAT DEBATE

1. John G. Stackhouse Jr., *Finally Feminist: A Pragmatic Christian Understanding of Gender: Why Both Sides Are Wrong—and Right* (Grand Rapids: Baker, 2005), 23. Dr. Stackhouse goes on to say, "No one I had read (and I had read quite a few) could put all the relevant texts together into a single, finished puzzle with no pieces left over, with none manufactured to fill in gaps, and with none forced into place. I began to recall, with mounting excitement, how champions of one view typically ignored or explained away the leading texts of champions of other views."

2. Three New Testament texts lie at the heart of the debate:

> For God is not a God of disorder but of peace. As in all the congregations of the saints, women should remain silent in the churches. They are not allowed to speak, but must be in submission, as the Law says. If they want to inquire about something, they should ask their own husbands at home; for it is disgraceful for a woman to speak in the church. (1 Corinthians 14:33–35)

> A woman should learn in quietness and full submission. I do not permit a woman to teach or to have authority over a man; she must be silent. (1 Timothy 2:11–12)

> There is neither Jew nor Greek, slave nor free, male nor female, for you are all one in Christ Jesus. (Galatians 3:28)

3. See www.barna.org/barna-update/article/17-leadership/304-number-of-female-senior-pastors-in-protestant-churches-doubles-in-past-decade?q=church+attendance.

4. Acts 5:1–11. Sapphira's story is strategically sandwiched in between two confrontations between the apostles and Jewish religious officials in a crackdown to prevent the apostles from proclaiming the gospel of Jesus Christ. Twice, officials order them to stop. In the first encounter, "Peter and John replied, 'Do you think God wants us to obey you rather than him? We cannot stop telling about the wonderful things we

have seen and heard' " (Acts 4:19–20). In the second, "Peter and the apostles replied, 'We must obey God rather than any human authority' " (Acts 5:29). In between, Sapphira agrees to go along with her husband's scheme of generosity mingled with deceit. Within the patriarchal culture, where a husband's word is law and a wife is often powerless to go against him, you'd think her behavior would be excused. Yet Peter (who elsewhere teaches wives of unbelievers to submit to their husbands) is appalled by Sapphira's behavior and holds her personally accountable for her actions. Clearly, submission carries enormous responsibility, requiring us to use our minds, act with courage, and be ready to say "No!" To read more on submission, see "The Three Faces of Submission" in Carolyn Custis James, *The Gospel of Ruth: Loving God Enough to Break the Rules* (Grand Rapids: Zondervan, 2008), 157–171.

5. See Matthew 18:1–10; Mark 9:30–37; Luke 9:43–48 and Matthew 20:17–28; Mark 10:32–45.

6. David E. Garland, *Mark* (NIV Application Commentary; Grand Rapids: Zondervan, 1996), 367.

7. Daniel Brennan, *Sacred Unions, Sacred Passions: Engaging the Mystery of Friendship between Men and Women* (Elgin, IL: Faith Dance, 2010), 112.

8. Andy Crouch, *Culture Making: Recovering Our Creative Calling* (Downers Grove, IL: InterVarsity Press, 2008), 138.

9. Garland, *Mark*, 367.

10. William L. Lane, *Commentary on the Gospel of Mark* (New International Commentary on the New Testament; Grand Rapids: Eerdmans, 1974), 339.

CONCLUSION: WAKING THE SLEEPING GIANTESS

1. Frank Houghton, *Amy Carmichael of Dohnavur* (Fort Washington, PA: Christian Literature Crusade, n.d.), 85.

2. Ibid.

3. Richard Landes, "Y2K Hangover and the New Millenium," www .bu.edu/mille/people/rlpages/Y2Khangoverandnewmille.html

4. John Mosley, "Wondering about the 'Star of Wonder,' " 12/9/2008, www.msnbc.msn.com/id/3077385/.

5. Abigail Hauslohner, "Afghanistan: When Women Set Themselves on Fire," www.time.com/time/world/article/0,8599,2002340,00.html.

6. Abraham Kuyper, "Sphere Sovereignty," in James D. Bratt, *Abraham Kuyper: A Centennial Reader* (Grand Rapids: Eerdmans, 1993), 488.

7. Gary A. Haugen, *Good News about Injustice: A Witness of Courage in a Hurting World* (Carol Stream, IL: InterVarsity Press, 2009), 22.

8. Ibid., 22–23.

9. Ecclesiology is the part of theology that centers on what the Bible teaches about the church, the people of God, and what it means to be the body of Christ.

10. Anthropology is the part of theology that centers on what the Bible teaches about human beings — male and female.

11. Amy Wilson-Carmichael, *Things As They Are, Mission Work in Southern India* (London: Morgan and Scott, 1904), 233 (emphasis hers).

12. From the website of the Dohnavur Fellowship: www.amycarmichael .org/.

Share Your Thoughts

With the Author: Your comments will be forwarded to the author when you send them to *zauthor@zondervan.com*.

With Zondervan: Submit your review of this book by writing to *zreview@zondervan.com*.

Free Online Resources at
www.zondervan.com

Daily Bible Verses and Devotions: Enrich your life with daily Bible verses or devotions that help you start every morning focused on God. Visit www.zondervan.com/newsletters.

Free Email Publications: Sign up for newsletters on Christian living, academic resources, church ministry, fiction, children's resources, and more. Visit www.zondervan.com/newsletters.

Zondervan Bible Search: Find and compare Bible passages in a variety of translations at www.zondervanbiblesearch.com.

Other Benefits: Register to receive online benefits like coupons and special offers, or to participate in research.